ARTS OF
RUSSIA

ARTS OF RUSSIA

17th and 18th Centuries

ABRAAM L. KAGANOVICH

Translated from the Russian by James Hogarth

92 illustrations in colour

31 illustrations in black and white

THE WORLD PUBLISHING COMPANY CLEVELAND AND NEW YORK

PUBLISHER'S NOTE

This second volume of ARTS OF RUSSIA is concerned with the 17th and 18th centuries, taking up the tale from the earlier volume which dealt with Russian art from the origins to the end of the 16th century.

Although the Russian art of these two centuries is rather more familiar to us than the art of mediaeval Russia, it has been no less arduous a task to bring together the material required to illustrate this volume. We are, therefore, particularly grateful to all those who have helped us in our quest, whether in a private or in an official capacity.

We should like in the first place to thank Mr V. A. Ankudinov, President of the Directorate of Foreign Tourism attached to the Council of Ministers of the U.S.S.R., who has used the high authority of his office to give us every possible assistance.

We must also express our gratitude for the help and advice we have received from Mr B. Piotrovsky, Director of the Hermitage Museum, Leningrad; Mrs V. Berezina and Mr V. G. Lukonin, Keepers in that Museum; and M. B. Lossky, Conservateur of the Musée National du Château de Fontainebleau.

Finally our thanks are due to Mr V. Komolov, Director of Publications of the Novosti Press Agency, the Museum of Art and History, Geneva, and M. J. Goetelen for the material which they have so kindly made available to us.

I THE SEVENTEENTH CENTURY

The study of Russian art has made great strides in the years since the second world war. During these years many works by Russian artists and craftsmen have been collected, restored and carefully studied, and numerous books and articles have been published which throw fresh light on the history of Russian art. This is particularly true of mediaeval art, and it is also true of 18th century art. In these fields impressive progress has been made. All over Russia, in old churches and local museums, are large numbers of important works which are now being systematically collected and studied and are steadily supplementing the resources of the great museums. Much new light has also been thrown on the art of the 17th century, so that we are now in a position to define more accurately its particular aesthetic qualities.

In Russia the 17th century began with the stormy period known as the Time of Troubles, which had far-reaching effects on the economic and political, and consequently also on the spiritual, life of Russian society. After the death of Ivan the Terrible and the reign of Boris Godunov the country suffered further afflictions in the form of a disastrous harvest and a severe famine throughout the whole of Russia. Popular discontent led to risings against the boyars and landowners, and many peasants absconded from the estates to which they were bound. These stirrings of revolt in turn led the ruling classes of feudal society to enter into an agreement with the Poles under which they gained possession of Moscow, while the Swedes occupied the northern territories of Russia.

The famine, destruction and pillaging which accompanied this foreign occupation threatened the very existence of the kingdom, and life in the cities came almost to a standstill. In this fateful hour,

however, there developed a patriotic movement for the re-establishment of Russian independence and the expulsion of the foreign oppressors. The heroes of this movement were Kuzma Minin and Dmitry Pozharsky, who led a national rising against the enemy and succeeded in driving out the occupying forces and restoring some degree of order in the country; and in 1713 the young Michael Romanov, the founder of the last dynasty to rule over Russia, was elected Tsar.

The election of a Tsar did not, however, mean that the country's difficulties were over. The turmoil of the early years of the century had far-reaching consequences and set powerful social forces in motion. These years of constant struggle against internal troubles and external enemies formed the character of the Russian people, strengthening their national awareness and their consciousness of their own strength.

An event of first-rate importance during this period was the union of the Ukraine with Russia, which increased the extent and enhanced the importance of the kingdom. Meanwhile the Russians were actively engaged in winning Siberia and the northern territories, developing their trade, building ships and sending a variety of expeditions to the East — leading to the discovery of Kamchatka, the Kuriles, the straits between Asia and America, etc.

The growing might of Muscovy was now increasingly borne in on the countries of the West. In the 17th century relationships between Russia and these countries became closer, and trading links were established with many other countries, ranging as far afield as India and the distant land of China.

Wars, social unrest, schism within the Church, peasant risings, calamitous destruction and the rapid rebirth of new towns from the ashes of the old: this was the pattern of the century, which gave a special vigour and dynamism to the life of Russia in this period. Entirely new impulses made themselves felt in the social framework which had persisted throughout so many centuries, giving fresh direction to many aspects of Russian life.

Life, indeed, was not easy for the Russians of the 17th century. The age-old struggle to wrest a living from nature, the constant fight against the oppressions of the Tsars and boyars, and the wars with the foreign aggressors who sought to occupy the soil of Russia — all these things strengthened the Russian character and gave it a distinctive stamp. The difficulties with which the Russian people had perpetually to contend developed a characteristic shrewdness and spirit of enterprise, a courage which shrank from nothing, and an indefatigable energy. In spite of all their tribulations the people of Russia preserved their optimism, their independence and their belief in the beauty of the world which surrounded them. And these characteristics inevitably influenced their art: the complex, troubled and contradictory history of the 17th century was faithfully reflected in the work of both folk and professional artists, which was as complex and variable as the life of the period which it portrayed.

The art of the 17th century has been the subject of very

varying judgments by Russian critics. Some writers regard it as the time of flowering of the older Russian art; others as a period of decline which saw "the dying out of all the arts of ancient Russia". These are extreme views, reflecting the aesthetic principles of particular scholars. But in our own day, in the light of intensive study of the culture of the period and detailed examination of its painting, graphic art and architecture, it is possible to make a profounder and more objective assessment of 17th century Russian art and to recognise both its qualities and its defects; and we can now identify more clearly the new features which give so much of the work of this period its own particular charm.

The 17th century surpassed all earlier periods in the abundance and magnificence of the architecture it produced and in the unprecedented development of monumental painting of remarkable originality

and richness of form. We can at once distinguish two opposing trends in the art of this century. On the one hand it was still under the influence of the old mediaeval traditions; on the other it was developing realistic tendencies which were entirely new. In this sense the culture of the period is clearly transitional, though at the same time it has a distinctive character of its own, which is clearly recognisable in the work it produced. The development of 17th century art is commonly referred to as a process of "secularisation"; and this term accurately expresses the declining influence of Church dogma and the assertion of lay influences which were more closely in touch with the circumstances of everyday life. This is true of Russian culture as a whole, and of all the various genres of figurative art. It is very necessary to understand this process, since it gives us an essential insight into the character of Russian art in this period and the pattern of its development. This secularisation becomes particularly evident in the second half of the century.

The occupation of Moscow by the Poles led to the destruction and desecration of its numerous churches. The old timber-built city suffered heavy damage; large areas were burned down, and many streets and squares were left abandoned and desolate. "Then the tall houses of the city, resplendent with many beauties, were destroyed," records the chronicler; "everything was consumed by fire, and all the churches with their fair domes were utterly brought to ruin by the foul hands of the enemy." The same fate befell other towns which lay in the path of the invaders. Then the upsurge of national feeling which followed the Time of Troubles led to vigorous building activity throughout the country and particularly, of course, in the capital. This rebuilding completely altered the appearance of many towns: new centres were created, whole layouts were changed, new fortifications were built and numbers of new religious and secular buildings were erected.

All this new building was strictly controlled. A special "Masonry Board" was established to take charge of the whole building programme, arrangements were made for the training of architects and builders, a standard size of brick was prescribed, and so on. All this ensured that the rebuilding was carried out in a properly planned and organised way and was recognised as an enterprise of supreme national importance. The chaotic huddle of building which had been characteristic of earlier towns now began to disappear, and the wider problems of town planning received consideration for the first time and were solved in ways which took account of the requirements of the whole architectural complex. Much of the new building was in stone and brick — another indication of the general improvement in the standard of architecture.

The rich store of experience built up by each successive generation of builders was now handed on to the next. We know the names of many of the leading architects of the 17th century — Antip Konstantinov, Bazhen Ogurtsov, the Startsev brothers, Averky Mokeev, Pavel Potekhin, Yakov Bukhvostov and many others—whose work gives evidence of remarkable talent and professional skill.

A characteristic feature of 17th century architecture is the emergence of local schools — in Moscow, Ryazan, Yaroslavl, Rostov, Suzdal and other towns — each with its own distinctive style, its own individual conception of architectural form. Although all these schools had a certain community of style and technique, each of them had its own specific characteristics. In spite of these local variations, however, the distinctive features which are common to all 17th century architecture are readily perceptible and can be recognised at a glance.

The religious buildings of the early years of the century show little trace of novelty. The planning and decoration of the churches is very similar to that of earlier buildings. As examples of the work of this period we may take the Church of the Protection of the Virgin in Rubtsovo (1626) and the Church of St Nicholas in Yaroslavl (1621), in both of which the general composition and decoration are completely traditional. In these early years of the century we see a continuation of the trend away from the tent roof *(shatër)*.

In the second quarter of the century new features begin to assert themselves, and the distinctive features of 17th century architecture begin to take shape. The tendency is now towards an assymetric layout: the main structure of the church is surrounded by a whole range of chapels, porches, staircases, galleries, passages, flights of steps, and so on, creating an effect of great variety and picturesqueness. Whereas earlier churches had as a rule formed a complete architectural whole, often standing by itself, the new buildings bore a much closer spatial relationship to their surroundings. The accent was now laid on the three-dimensional plastic quality of the architecture, and the buildings of the period are remarkable for their complex decorative structure and striking effect.

We may take as an example the Church of the Trinity in Nikitniki, Moscow, built between 1623 and 1653. The high square tower with its domes, the two chapels, the porch and the bell-tower combine to produce a building of great picturesque effect: an effect which is enhanced by the *kokoshniki* (decorative gable-heads), the pairs of colonnettes, the brick mouldings and the use of polychrome decoration.

Another typical building of this period is the Church of the Prophet Elijah in Yaroslavl (1647-50)

(Plate p. 41), a five-domed structure to which a number of chapels, flights of steps and porches are annexed. The octagonal bell-tower with a tent roof and one of the chapels, also with a tent roof, give the church an impressive monumentality and dignity.

A characteristic feature of the churches of this period is that their external appearance often bears no relation to their internal structure. The exterior tends to become a mere superficial decoration applied by the architects to achieve an elegant effect; and the interior is sometimes composed of a number of separate elements which are not combined to form a unified whole.

In the middle of the century the Church began to take exception to this widespread use of decorative ornament as a manifestation of the secularisation of Russian culture. The Patriarch Nikon, that great protagonist of the policy of the Church, whose aim was to establish the pre-eminence of the ecclesiastical over the secular power, laid down his own architectural canons. Religious architecture must demonstrate by its magnificence and monumentality, and by its grandiose scale, the strength and authority of the Church. The large monasteries built by Nikon — the Monastery of the Cross, the Iberian Monastery and the Monastery of the New Jerusalem — were designed to exemplify these new requirements. The cathedral in the Monastery of the New Jerusalem, with its huge tent roof and rotunda, was a building of particular magnificence. It was not possible, however, to turn back the course of architectural development, and even the Monastery of the New Jerusalem showed clear evidence of the quest for decorative effect, which was enhanced by the lavish use of coloured tiles and the disposition of the subsidiary elements built on to the main structure.

The buildings of the mid 17th century began to show a clearer and more logical arrangement of the separate parts, though without abandoning the lavish decoration which had become general. The interiors of the churches were as richly decorated as ever, resplendent with their brightly coloured mural paintings, the rich gilding and carving of the iconostases, and the silver and gilt frames of the icons.

The architecture of the last quarter of the century was of particular individuality, in the characteristic style known as "Moscow baroque" or the "Naryskhin style", after the family of that name on whose estates the most striking examples of the style were built. The churches of this period now showed a more logical sense of layout: the main structure of the building was clearly defined, the central part of the church being given a distinct vertical emphasis, while the subsidiary elements lost their earlier independence and were related to the main structure.

The interiors of these churches are remarkable for their richly carved iconostases, which surpass anything previously achieved in this field. The most striking features of these churches, however, are their exteriors, with their dynamic lines, their abundance of relief ornament, and the intricacy and elaboration of their carving. The "wondrous ornament" for which they were famed, the liveliness of the modelling and the use of white stone are the distinguishing features of this style. Other important elements are the polychrome decoration and the glazed tiles with which the external walls were decorated (*Plate p. 14*).

A striking example of this style is provided by the Church of the Protection of the Virgin at Fili (1693-94). The octagons of decreasing size superimposed on one another to form the tower, the flights of steps which flank the main structure, and the profusion of decoration combine to create an impression of lightness and grace. The church fits beautifully into its surroundings, and the elegance of the detailing and contrasting pattern of colour show a high degree of architectural refinement which demonstrates the builders' ability to preserve and develop the native traditions of Russian architecture.

In spite of the large numbers of stone buildings in the towns of the 17th century the bulk of the building in towns — and of course even more so in the country — continued to be in timber. Wood was the cheapest and most readily available material, easy to work and familiar through many centuries of use; and the people of Russia were reluctant to abandon the material they loved so

15

well. The buildings erected in this period are unsurpassed for their impeccable sense of proportion, their delicacy of finish and their profusion of carved ornament.

Their builders understood the "soul" of the wood, the beauty and variety of its structure, its colouring, and the characteristics of the different timbers. They were able not only to plan the structure of a building and achieve an exact interpretation of its function, but also to endow it with outstanding aesthetic qualities.

Russian timber churches are light and graceful, usually small but sometimes of considerable size, and almost always of high artistic quality. The soaring upward movement of their bell-towers, the graceful domes surmounted by crosses, and the design and decoration of the windows and doors bear witness to a profound and subtle sense of plastic beauty. How striking, too, is the festive grace of the iconostases, with their profusion of carved ornament, combining vegetable motifs, twisted columns and openwork tracery into a complex decorative pattern! The icons and the scenes from the Scriptures emerge with increased elegance and effect from this riot of painted and gilded carving. Even in the very smallest churches the iconostases are authentic works of art. In other types of building, too, we find wood used with great effect — in town mansions built by skilled craftsmen and in peasants' huts, which were frequently also decorated with carved ornament. And these are traditions which are still alive in our own day.

The houses built in towns were frequently of two or three stories, with a high roof and projecting porches decorated with carving. A striking example of this type of building was the famous royal palace in the village of Kolomenskoe near Moscow, built between 1667 and 1681. This consisted of seven separate buildings linked by passages into a single whole, each part of the structure — which in places was of three or four stories — having its own roof. The external staircases, the corridors, the galleries and the windows were richly ornamented with carving, giving the whole building a picturesque and decorative effect. The internal walls were covered with ornamental and pictorial painting. The palace, a building unique of its kind, had a life of something like a century before it fell into a state of dilapidation and had to be demolished.

Wooden churches with tent roofs were also built in the 17th century, the high "tent" being erected on a square base. Most of these were in the north of the country: in central Russia the preference was for large stone-built churches, cubic in shape, with either a single dome or five domes above a hipped roof.

A new form of architecture now developed to meet the need for commercial and industrial buildings. In Archangel, for example, Dmitry Startsev built a huge complex of commercial buildings, the Gostinny Dvor (Bazaar, Market), with a total length of something like a quarter of a mile, protected by a stone wall with square towers at intervals. Commercial buildings of a new type were also erected in Moscow and other towns.

An example of the large-scale development of stone building in the 17th century is provided by the ancient city of Novgorod, where a new Voivode's Palace in stone was built in replacement of an earlier timber structure. The Palace consisted of a whole complex of buildings, including the Voivode's Residence, churches, towers and ancillary buildings.

The work was carried out on instructions from Moscow that "in future the building should be stout and strong, so that boyars and voivodes might dwell in their residences of stone without constraint or difficulty". The whole palace complex and certain other buildings in Novgorod were erected by an architect sent from Moscow, Efimov.

The process of town development in the 17th century can be followed in the Kremlin of Rostov (1670-83) *(Plates pp. 16-20)*, which provides a striking demonstration of the progress made in the art of town planning and of the high degree of skill achieved by the builders of the period. The old Cathedral of the Dormition was left outside the walls, and the new buildings were laid out round a grand courtyard and garden in the centre of the Kremlin. The principal building in the Kremlin was the audience chamber, the White Hall. It is significant that the new Kremlin was not merely an austere defensive structure, as its predecessor had been, but resembled an elegant mansion picturesquely situated on the banks of Lake Nero.

Typical specimens of the civil architecture of this period are provided by the monastery buildings, and particularly by the refectories. As an example we may take the refectory of the Monastery of the Trinity and St Sergius *(Plates pp. 23, 24)*. This huge vaulted room still makes a powerful impression with its size and spaciousness. Its most striking feature, however, is the design of the external walls, which are remarkable for their sense of proportion and the richness of their architectural detail. This gives the whole building an unusual elegance, and its beauty and impressiveness are increased by the columns which frame the windows, the frieze of scallop-shell mouldings, and the general richness of colouring. The refectory of the Simonov Monastery (1677-80) is another typical building of this period.

Within our own day Moscow has enormously increased in size.

New streets and parks have been laid out and new residential areas have grown up, so that the whole face of the old city has been transformed. Many of the older buildings have either disappeared altogether or been reconstructed. Fortunately, however, the mass of new building has not entirely obliterated the fascinating remains of the past, which have survived to provide a lasting reminder of the achievement and the distinctive characteristics of Russian art. The picturesque old churches of Moscow, its stone-built mansions, its defensive walls and towers give the city its particular colouring and its special charm, recalling the history of Russia's ancient capital and the glorious traditions of its art and architecture. The 17th century thus played a large part in the creation of the distinctive atmosphere of Moscow as we know it today.

In this period great changes took place in the general pattern and layout of the city. The monasteries were rebuilt, the old winding lanes were replaced by straight streets, timber building was forbidden in the central area, and the new churches which were now erected were designed to fit into their particular place in the plan of their district and of the city as a whole. There was a considerable development of building in stone, not only for churches but also for dwelling houses and public buildings. We know

from foreigners who visited Moscow in the 17th century of the magnificence of the city's architecture. "We marvelled at their beauty," writes one of these visitors, Paul of Aleppo; "at the ornament, the solidity, the fine architecture and the elegance of the buildings, their great number of windows and of columns with carved decoration, and the abundance of painting in many colours, both within and without: indeed it seemed that the buildings were in truth decorated with pieces of many-coloured marble and delicately formed mosaics." This statement by a foreign observer provides convincing evidence that Moscow was a town of outstanding beauty and magnificence, a large and populous city which made an overwhelming impression on any visitor.

The town residences of the boyars and merchants had a characteristic layout of their own, usually consisting of an enclosed area within which were a grand courtyard and the mansion itself, often comprising two separate parts joined by a passage. Behind this were domestic offices, a garden and a kitchen-garden. The properties of the richer citizens might include a private church. The whole complex formed an independent unit which nevertheless fitted into the general pattern of the town: indeed these mansions, standing by themselves in a mantle of greenery, added their own distinctive touch of picturesqueness to the urban scene.

The most important group of buildings in Moscow was in its splendid Kremlin *(Plates pp. 26, 27)*. With the Kremlin were associated all the most important events in the history of Russia, all the most glorious pages of its past. It was the very heart of the Russian state, the incarnation of its power and

authority. And in the striking and distinctive beauty of the Kremlin, the buildings within its walls, and the treasures which it contains, we can sense the spiritual greatness and the artistic gifts of the men who created them.

The history of the Kremlin goes back to times of remote antiquity. It was already established as the centre of Moscow by the middle of the 12th century, and the 14th century saw the building of the stone Cathedrals of the Archangel Michael and the Dormition, together with the stone walls and towers of its ramparts. After the famous Battle of Kulikovo in 1380, when the Tatar hordes were routed and Moscow became the capital of the Russian state, the Kremlin underwent an intensive process of rebuilding. For this purpose some of the leading Italian architects of the day were called in — men like Aristotele Fioravanti, Marco Ruffo, Pietro Solari and Alevisio the Second. The Kremlin was enlarged, its walls and towers were strengthened,

the cathedrals were reconstructed and the Palace of Facets was built. At this period, too, the tall watch-tower known as Ivan the Great's Bell-tower was built (completed in 1600).

The Kremlin suffered grievously during the troubled period at the beginning of the 17th century. Many of the buildings fell into a state of dilapidation, or were destroyed or burned down. After the Time of Troubles the country began to recover, and considerable building operations were undertaken: the stone palaces of the Tsars, the *Terems*, were built, and the defensive towers were reconstructed *(Plate p. 25)*. It was in this period that the Kremlin took on the appearance which is familiar today.

Even after the capital of the country was transferred to the banks of the Neva in the 18th century building continued in the Kremlin, and the churches and the ancient walls, hallowed by the heroic memories of the past, retained all their significance for the people of Russia.

The walls and towers of the Kremlin as we know them today were the result of a rebuilding between 1485 and 1495 which provided the citadel of Moscow with powerful defences against any attacker; but the buildings within the walls were by no means confined to those associated with the Kremlin's defensive function. The walls of the Kremlin are 20 feet thick and stand over 60 feet high; they have a total circuit of over 2400 yards, punctuated by twenty towers which enhance the beauty and impressive-

ness of the whole complex. The 70 acres enclosep within the walls contain a great variety of historic buildings, both palaces and churches, making the Kremlin a veritable museum of Russian culture.

The many-storied Borovitsky Tower, built in 1490 by Pietro Antonio Solari, was given a high tent roof in the 17th century. The wall above the River Moskva was reinforced by the building of the Blagoveshchensky, Taynitsky, Petrovsky and other towers; and the severe Beklemishevsky Tower at the south-east corner, built by Marco Ruffo in 1487, was heightened.

The finest of the towers is the Spassky, built by Solari in 1491, which combines monumentality and elegance, severity of line and graceful openwork detailing. In 1625 Bazhen Ogurtsov and the English clockmaker Christopher Galloway added a tent roof and a clock. The niches in the upper part of the tower at one time contained pieces of sculpture, but these were later destroyed.

The 17th century made fundamental changes in the architecture of the towers. The increase in their height completely altered their character, and the soaring tent roofs gave them a distinctively Russian appearance. It is now difficult to imagine the Kremlin towers without their spires, which give the squat defensive architecture of the original towers an air of triumphant elegance.

The architecture of the 17th century was a confident and vigorous art. In spite of its rather limited thematic range it was a clear affirmation of its creators' striving for beauty and perfection. As it developed it extended its range, facing and solving many complex problems of planning and design, achieving its own form of synthesis with painting and sculpture, and grappling successfully with structural problems of great complexity. A significant feature of Russian architecture was its intimate contact with folk art, which gave it a flavour and picturesqueness of its own and enabled it to express the joyous assertion of human values which is so strikingly displayed in many aspects of Russian art in the 17th century.

The painting of the 17th century, a compound of many different elements, has still been very inadequately studied, having — as sometimes happens in the world of scholarship — been neglected in favour of other fields of more immediate interest. The result is that many aspects of the remarkable heritage left to us by the 17th century have not received the attention they deserve and are still an unknown quantity. The circumstances in which many fine pieces of painting were executed remain obscure, and the names of the artists who painted some of the magnificent icons of the period are still unknown. In spite of these deficiencies, however, the significance of the 17th century in the history of painting is now generally recognised; the achievements of the Russian artists of this period are now appreciated at their true worth, and we are accordingly able to assess the

importance of their work, and in particular of their painting, in the historical development of Russian art as a whole.

Seventeenth century painting shows evidence of the changes whick took place in the outlook of the artists, of their search for new means of expression, of their departure from the older traditions. It demonstrates clearly the characteristic features of this period of transition between the Middle Ages and modern times. The representation of the real world and of real people now became the principal theme of art. The new interest in nature, in portraiture and in the representation of scenes from everyday life is evidence of a fresh artistic trend — a trend which of course reflected a change in circumstances and in human attitudes.

In this period the asceticism of the Middle Ages was faced with a decisive challenge; and the intensity of the conflict is shown clearly by the controversy to which it gave rise in the field of aesthetics.

The process which began in the 17th century was continued and largely completed in the following century; and the art of the 18th century is thus the result of a rich and complex earlier development.

In the painting of the 17th century we can readily discern two trends which determine its character and give the period its own particular individuality. On the one hand there was a quest for new forms,

untrammelled by the dogmatic traditions of the past, secular in character and closer to real life; on the other there was a tendency to maintain established conventions, to erect the traditions of the past into a dogma, to declare their absolute validity and to defend them against the malign influences of the contemporary world. These two conflicting tendencies in art and literature were the determining factors in the evolution of Russian culture during this period. On occasion the conflict developed into an acute controversy, a collision between differing aesthetic attitudes, and sometimes indeed extended beyond the province of art to take on overtones of social conflict.

A new artistic school now developed in protest against the age-old traditionalism and abstractness of religious painting. An important part in the development of the new trend was played by the influence of western European art, with its realism, its closer reflection of everyday reality.

The leaders of this new school were the icon-painter Simon Ushakov, one of the leading Russian artists of the century, and Iosif Vladimirov, who campaigned vigorously for a fundamental change in artistic principles and practice.

A document of outstanding importance in the aesthetic controversy was Vladimirov's famous *Treatise on Icon-painting*, which gave unequivocal expression to the new principles and the new function which art was to serve, and set out the distinctive aesthetic creed of the period. The *Treatise* reflects the clash between different views on the nature and objectives of art which was then engaging the minds of artists. Vladimirov attacks the ignorant icon-painters who "do not understand what is bad and what is good: they hold to ideas that are out of date and attribute a special virtue to those things that have long since fallen into decline and decay." Vladimirov also takes his stand against obsolete traditions, against outdated symbolism, against the conventionalised schematism of the older school of art, against anything that ran counter to the new ideas of the time. It is significant, however, that in relation to western European art and its achievements Vladimirov and other 17th century artists were very far from being mere imitators and by no means set up the art of the West as a model to be copied. What was at issue was the secular content of art, and above all the trend towards realism which appealed so strongly to the foremost Russian artists of the day. The features in foreign art which interested Vladimirov were not only the realistic treatment of religious subjects but the use of purely secular themes — the portraits of ordinary human beings and the artists' ability to "represent all manner of objects and events in their pictures, depicting them as they are in real life." We can see this trend at work in the genre scenes so characteristic of Russian art, of which the Yaroslavl paintings provide some striking examples, on themes taken from everyday life.

Vladimirov inveighs against the commercially produced icons of inferior quality which circulated in large numbers in the remotest parts of the country, constituting "a profanation and a mockery" of true art. The central problem with which he is concerned, however, is the artist's relationship to the subjects he represents. He attacks the adherents of the old conventional style of icon-painting. "Where did these senseless lovers of tradition discover the injunction to paint the figures of saints in this unchanging fashion, always with dark and swarthy faces?" he asks. His *Treatise* was a call to abandon the conventionality of the traditional style and be guided by reality and commonsense.

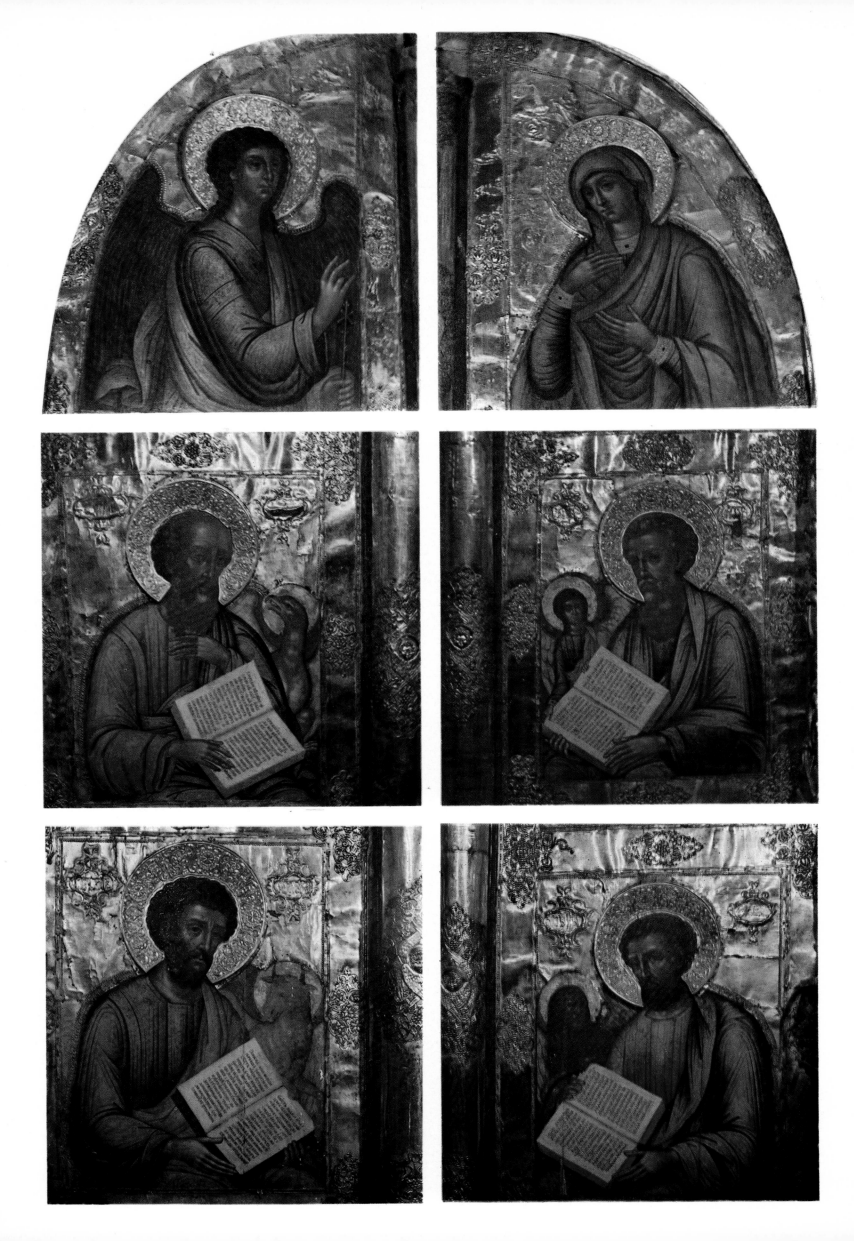

The effect of flatness which the older style demanded, the conventional attitudes and colouring, the use of allegorical symbolism — all the accepted features which represented a departure from reality were subjected to criticism and called in question. The theme which runs through the whole of Vladimirov's *Treatise* is the demand for naturalism in the representation of the human figure. Painting must seek to reproduce all the light and shade of reality rather than to achieve an artificial flatness and uniformity. In similar vein Simon Ushakov, in his *Word to the Lover of Icon-painting*, exalts the art of painting by comparing it with a mirror which must faithfully reflect the appearance of the external world.

Not unnaturally these new aesthetic ideas encountered fierce opposition from the supporters of the older ways. The principal advocate of the immutability of the church tradition in the field of art was the Archpriest Avvakum. The controversy became involved with the wider question of the relationship between Church and State — the increase of secular authority on the one hand and the Church's strenuous endeavour to maintain its privileges and its influence on the other. And the difficulties were aggravated at this period by the schism within the Church, associated as it was with the social unrests of the day.

Great changes were now taking place in the cultural life of Russia. An interest in secular education was spreading ever more widely throughout the population, particularly among the nobles and townsfolk. Many people in Moscow were becoming increasingly interested in Western culture and science, and increasingly critical of the backwardness of Russian life and of the conservatism which set so much store by outdated traditions. Literature now began to show an active concern with secular themes and increasingly lost its theological character. An interest in the details of everyday life and the personalities of real people is found side by side with accounts of the lives of saints, and some memoirs of the period are remarkable for their colourful language and exactness of observation. We can observe the same process at work in the figurative arts. Nevertheless we may still note a certain reserve in this respect, and sometimes even an indication of contradictory tendencies. Even the most prominent artists of the period could not afford to commit themselves wholeheartedly to these revolutionary changes, and even while making a fundamental break with tradition felt bound to follow it in certain respects. But the admission of themes reflecting the pulsating life of the everyday world into the established compositional stereotypes of painting was the first stage in the collapse of the mediaeval aesthetic system.

The changes which took place in painting during the 17th century showed themselves in a slackening of the hold exercised by symbolism, a preference for narrative subjects, an increasing tendency for pictures to tell a story. No doubt all these new ideas were still on a fairly modest scale, and were not by any means to be found in every field of art; but it was the emergence of these trends which gave the period its distinctive character.

In the first half of the century icon-painting was still in many respects under the influence of the older traditions. This was a consequence of the very nature of the genre and the part it played in the life of the period. Nevertheless the striking feature of 17th century icon-painting is its increasing concern with the phenomena of everyday life. At first this process develops cautiously, as we can see from the icon of "The Council of St John the Baptist" (1629, Tretyakov Gallery) or the "Trinity" (Tretyakov Gallery), in which the traditionalism of the composition and the treatment of the figures are strongly reminiscent of the work of earlier periods.

The new spirit is unmistakable, however, in the icon of the "Virgin of Bogolyubovo" (Tretyakov Gallery), painted in the first half of the century. The figures of the Tsarevich Dmitry and the saints with hands extended in prayer who are standing in front of the Virgin, their faces set in grief and an appeal for help, achieve a genuine expressiveness.

An important contribution was made to the art of icon-painting in the first quarter of the 17th century by the "Stroganov school", so called after the wealthy family of merchants and industrialists whose icon-painting workshops produced icons of a very distinctive type.

The Stroganov icons are notable for exquisite refinement of draughtsmanship, painting technique and composition. Clearly they were intended for private use rather than public display. Small in size, and each devoted to a particular religious theme, they depict delicately drawn little figures with elongated bodies and tiny heads. The attitudes are elegant and indeed rather mannered, and the placing of the figures is designed for ornamental effect. The same themes are frequently repeated. Looking at these icons, we are often reminded of miniatures.

The characters in the Stroganov icons are clad in elegant and brightly coloured garments. They move lightly and gracefully, seeming barely to touch the ground, and are often depicted against a background of tree-covered hills. The painters used a delicately drawn line and a light wash of colour to suggest the elegance and refinement of the figures. The colour scheme is based on the use of pinkish and greyish-green tones with touches of red and with gold lettering. The style shows extreme meticulousness, reminiscent of the delicacy of the jeweller's craft.

The icons of the Stroganov school are usually on narrative themes and are full of details from secular life. As examples of the style we may take such magnificent icons as "The Miracle of St Theodore Tiro" (Russian Museum) and certain works by the leading representative of the school, Prokopy Chirin, such as his "St Nikita the Warrior" (Tretyakov Gallery) and "St John the Warrior" (Russian Museum). These works show all the most characteristic features of the delicate and individual Stroganov style.

It is worth remarking that we can get a direct impression of this style from the work of the craftsmen of Palekh, who have preserved the traditions of the Stroganov school into our own day.

The influence of the Stroganov school was still powerfully felt throughout the first half of the century, as is shown by the exquisite refinement of finish and miniature-like painting technique found in many icons of this period. As an example of this we may take an icon of the "Metropolitan Aleksey" (1640s, Tretyakov Gallery), the composition and technique of which are very reminiscent of the Stroganov school. In the icons produced in Moscow in this period, however, the influence of the Stroganov school gradually declines and gives place to a style of greater austerity; the meticulous finish disappears, the figures become simpler and less consciously elegant. This style is exemplified in the iconostasis of the Church of the Laying On of the Veil in the Kremlin, which shows extreme coldness and fussiness in the treatment of the figures, in spite of the expressiveness of the new manner.

In the middle of the 17th century the main icon-painting centre in Russia was the Armoury in Moscow, where artists not only from Moscow but from other Russian towns were actively at work. The city thus became an important centre of painting, bringing together the finest artists of the day. Individual icon-painters now tended to work within very specialised fields, so that a number of artists were sometimes engaged on a single icon. In the middle of the century the Armoury was also a centre for other types of painters, whose work was in continually increasing demand. It was not, however, in any sense an association of independent artists: the painters were members of a highly organised corporation, with the same status and the same living and working conditions as other craftsmen. The Armoury was also in effect a large art school in which many gifted artists received their professional training.

There were significant variations in 17th century attitudes to icons. Those who were still attached to the older ideas regarded them purely as cult objects and objected to any departure from the accepted symbolism and the traditional patterns, while the more progressive elements in society, including

in particular the artists of the new school, sought to establish the icon as a work of art, a reflection of reality, an object of aesthetic value in its own right. This led to a clash of opposing views, and to an outburst of violent controversy and mutual recrimination. The characters depicted in icons must not resemble ordinary people, and the world they represented must not be a mere copy of the everyday world: this was the view of the Church, which was now opposed by the newer and more progressive school of aesthetic thought. The "senseless lovers of tradition" were faced with a new conception of the icon as a work of art. In an epistle addressed by Vladimirov to Simon Ushakov we find these solemn words: "Truth does not follow behind ignorant custom: ignorant custom must give way to truth." Ushakov gathered round him a group of like-minded artists — Zinovyev, Maksimov, Ulanov and Filantyev — whose work reflected a constant quest for new directions in painting.

Of particular interest in this connection is the work of Tikhon Filantyev, which can be judged from his icon of "St John the Forerunner" (1689, Tretyakov Gallery). The principal figure in this icon conveys a sense of genuine sorrow and is painted as a three-dimensional figure of flesh and blood in the new spirit characteristic of the 17th century.

These reforming trends were found not only in Ushakov and his immediate associates. Many artists with the same urge to depart from the accepted mediaeval stereotypes and introduce some vitality into their figures were at work in other towns, beyond the reach of his influence. This new movement, this urge to breathe life into the abstractions sanctified by tradition, was clearly in accordance with the spirit of the age. Among the other artists who showed the same tendencies were Nikita Pavlovets, the painter of a "Trinity" (Russian Museum) and a "Mother of God" (Tretyakov Gallery), and Fëdor Zubov, who produced icons and paintings containing large numbers of figures which reveal the artist's acute observation of everyday life.

In the second half of the century we find icons representing the lives of saints, round the edges of which are small panels on religious themes, depicted with a lively sense of reality. The vigorous and expressive figures in these icons show a genuine sensibility, a striving to achieve a faithful rendering of the passions, the joys and the sufferings which make up human life.

The icons of Yaroslavl, which show the influence of mural painting, are of particular interest. They represent a wide range of incidents from the lives of saints, in which genre scenes and situations taken from real life are constantly recurring. The close connection between icon-painting and monumental painting can be seen from the icon of "The Miracle of the Icon of the Virgin of Fëdorovo" (Russian Museum), in which some of the scenes show figures engaged in the vigorous activity characteristic of mural paintings. In these Yaroslavl icons the principal figure is usually in the centre of the painting, with a variety of subsidiary scenes depicted behind him on a much smaller scale.

The icons of this period also show an interest in secular themes and in battle scenes representing real historical events. This interest is demonstrated in an icon of St Sergius of Radonezh, dating from the 1650s or 1660s, which contains a frieze representing the Battle of Kulikovo, full of lively incidents from the legend *(Plate p. 45)*. The clash of mounted warriors and the hand-to-hand melee are depicted with great vigour and circumstantial detail, as if designed to appeal to an interested and knowledgeable audience.

Monumental painting was perhaps even more strongly affected by the new ideas. The artist's interest in the workaday world and in his natural surroundings found readier expression in this type of painting than in the icons. This can be seen, for example, in the frescoes in the Princess's Monastery in Vladimir, in the paintings in the Moscow cathedrals, and elsewhere. Although maintaining the accepted compositional patterns, the artists enriched their design with themes taken from real life. The colour schemes of the mural paintings also underwent a change: even in the first half of the century bright greens, blues and

pinks are found, greatly enhancing the liveliness and brilliance of the painting. In the first half of the century much painting was done in the churches of Moscow. A typical example was the painting of the Cathedral of the Dormition in the Kremlin (1642-43), where the work was carried out under the direction of Ivan Paisein, Sidor Osipov, Mark Matveev and others. The composition of these paintings was entirely traditional — figures of the "Saviour not Made with Hands", "Lord of Hosts" and "The Almighty" in the domes, angels on the vaulting, and apostles, prophets, saintly warriors and church festivals on the piers. Unfortunately not all the painting of this period has survived, and much of it was restored at a considerably later period; but the 17th century work that has come down to us shows the sense of innovation and the elegance which is found in so much of the painting of this period.

The largest enterprise of the 1650s and 1660s was the decoration of the Archangel Cathedral in the Kremlin, the burial-place of the Tsars and Princes of Russia. The artists engaged on this work included Yakov Kazanets, Iosif Vladimirov, Simon Ushakov and Gury Nikitin. The paintings are mainly devoted to the Archangel Michael *(Plate pp. 38-39)*, the patron saint of the Princes of Russia, but also include figures of the Princes and Tsars themselves. They are dedicated to the glorification of the secular authority of the State in all its manifestations. Other typical examples of the work of the period were the frescoes in the Church of the Trinity at Nikitniki (Moscow), reproducing subjects taken from western European engravings — a new development in monumental painting. These subjects were considerably modified and given an entirely new significance; but the very fact that they were used at all is of interest.

Religious themes were now less prominent in the paintings than in an earlier period, their place being taken by subjects of secular concern and by an interest in terrestrial reality and ordinary life. The religious myth frequently took on the form of a historical tale, sometimes based on real life, sometimes frankly fabulous. The new themes were often used in the galleries and porches of churches, but increasingly played a part in the decoration of the churches themselves.

Moscow continued to be the main centre of monumental painting, but this type of painting flourished also in Yaroslavl, Vologda and Kostroma. The Yaroslavl paintings are masterpieces of 17th century art, with a vivid colouring and lively narrative quality which puts them in a class by themselves. The interiors of the Yaroslavl churches were overlaid with a rich pattern of decoration made up of the most variegated motifs, in a style which was quite new in Russian monumental painting. The walls were covered with small pictures, arranged in separate bands or registers, mostly showing scenes from ordinary life, which were often linked in a consecutive sequence. In these pictures stories from the Old and New Testaments were presented with great liveliness and in a simple and straightforward way — often in the form of a series of incidents from everyday life — so that their message was conveyed at once to the spectator.

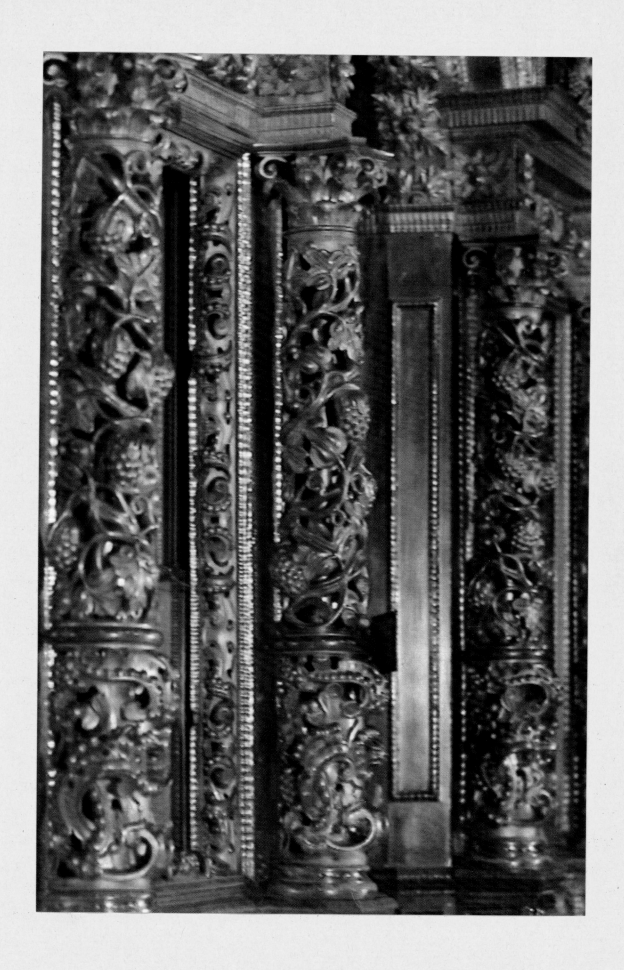

The most typical example of a Yaroslavl church decorated in the new style is the Church of the Prophet Elijah (1680) *(Plates pp. 41, 42, 46)*. The paintings were the work of a team of artists under the leadership of Gury Nikitin and Sila Savin, who had previously worked in Moscow, Rostov and other towns.

The upper part of the church is decorated with frescoes on entirely traditional themes, but the five bands of painting in the lower part contain a well-known series of narrative scenes in which the religious subject matter becomes of secondary importance compared with the lively and entertaining representation of incidents from real life. In depicting the story of Adam and Eve and their expulsion from Paradise' for example, the artists set their characters in a background which has clearly been taken from life, and are concerned to achieve an accurate representation of the natural surroundings, of real animals and birds, and of architectural details.

The most interesting series of paintings is the cycle devoted to the lives of the prophets Elijah and Elisha, containing a sequence of vividly depicted scenes in which stormy seas alternate with peaceful rural landscapes, the prophets rub shoulders with ordinary country folk, and representations of miracles are found side by side with scenes from everyday life. As an example we may take the magnificent fresco showing Elisha restoring the Shunammite's son to life, in which the main action becomes secondary to the picture of a harvesting scene *(Plate p. 42)*. We see the reapers gathering the rye, clad in blue and pink garments and wielding sickles. Their attitudes and movements, the yellow corn and the trees in the background build up a picture which is clearly painted from life. It was only in the 17th century that a subject of this kind, treated with such remarkable realism, could have found its way on to the walls of a church. And indeed scenes from everyday life are of frequent occurrence in 17th century painting. The Church of the Prophet Elijah, for example, also contains pictures of ploughing, house-building, and many similar subjects. The frescoes in this church are also notable for the beauty and elegance of the principal figures and the important part played by ornament, which is woven into the very fabric of the narrative.

No less typical of the period is the Church of St John the Forerunner in Tolchkovo (1695), which was decorated by a group of artists under the leadership of Dmitry Plekhanov. Notwithstanding the austerity of the subject matter and its treatment in comparison with the paintings in the Church of the Prophet Elijah, these paintings too are striking examples of the new style, the artists' new relationship to their subject matter and their lively imagination. In the scenes representing the chastisement of sinners the artists achieve a powerful effect and a strikingly lifelike rendering of

the figures. The pictures of the woman who has murdered her child, the Boat of the Godless and the expulsion of sinners are of great dramatic force, and the representations of the Last Judgment, crowded with figures of devils and monsters, the flames of Hell and the wretched sinners, reflect all the luxuriance of the folk imagination.

The bright pink and blue tones of the Yaroslavl frescoes created a variegated decorative pattern of extreme elegance which enhanced the richness and splendour of the churches. The paintings depicted real characters, often clad in the ordinary garments of the day as worn by peasants or boyars; but the artists also showed an interest in distant and exotic lands which was expressed in a variety of fantastic representations. Some of the paintings were on fabulous themes, appealing to men's imagination and their urge to comprehend the vastness and variety of the world. On the other hand the Yaroslavl frescoes tended to lack the severe monumentality which had been characteristic of the mural painting of the previous century. This is seen particularly in a failure to subordinate the painting to the architectural pattern of the interior; frequently, indeed, the painting bore no relationship to the architecture and became a mere decorative overlay. The pictures themselves, however, gave expression to themes of universal interest, and the composition as a whole was so striking and impressive that they achieved a powerful effect. They depicted a complex and many-sided world, a world which sometimes seemed remote from the observer but gradually developed into a clearly realised picture of reality. In this respect the paintings were very characteristic of their century, exemplifying the distinctive features of its artistic philosophy.

With their optimism, their feeling for reality and their profound novelty, the Yaroslavl frescoes inevitably influenced the work of other artists. In consequence we find a certain similarity between the Yaroslavl painting and the decoration of churches in other towns, an identity of artistic approach and a community of style. Typical examples of the painting of the period are found, for instance, in churches at Borisoglebsk — e.g., the frescoes in the Romanov Cathedral — and at Suzdal and Vologda. These show the same narrative manner and the same interest in secular themes as we find at Yaroslavl.

The notable feature of 17th century monumental painting is the dynamic force of the composition. In their striving to paint as complete a picture as possible of all the manifold activities of human life, the artists not only unfolded their narrative in a series of separate scenes, each one leading on to the next, but also — in striking contrast to the painting of earlier centuries — liked to represent their figures in violent movement, in bold foreshortening, in constant restless activity.

It remains true, however, that although the artists' eagerness to depict scenes from everyday life and to tell a story reflected their desire to apprehend as fully as possible the world which surrounded them, their treatment of the human figure was still in many respects traditional. It was still beyond their power to portray man's inner nature, his mind and spirit and character. This was to be the achievement of a later period in the history of Russian art.

The most important artist of the second half of the 17th century was Simon Ushakov (1626-86), a craftsman of outstanding professional skill who enjoyed great reputation and authority, and whose works give us the fullest expression of the characteristic features of the period. In addition to his creative work he is known as a theoretical writer. Standing as he did above the narrower interests of different groups and schools, he can be regarded as the leader of the artistic movement of the century.

Of his origin nothing is known. After many years of productive work in the Armoury he was raised to the ranks of the nobility, an honour only rarely accorded to artists. He was skilled in a wide range of crafts — drawing, engraving, icon-painting and monumental painting — and was in charge of the execution of the most important paintings of the period, in the Cathedral of the Dormition and the Archangel Cathedral in the Kremlin.

One of Ushakov's most popular icons is his "Saviour not Made with Hands" (1657, Tretyakov Gallery), a representation of Christ's head on the Vernicle. The subject was a common theme of icon-painting, but in Ushakov's hands it received a new interpretation. The novelty of the work lies in the method of treating Christ's face, in a markedly three-dimensional form which distinguishes it from other treatments of the same theme. The face is drawn with extreme restraint, with no effort to achieve expressiveness and no sense of inner movement; but in painting it the artist was clearly seeking to achieve the same realism as was appropriate in the portrayal of an ordinary human being.

We find the same qualities in Ushakov's icon of the "Trinity". While preserving the traditional structural pattern, he shows himself an innovator in the field of artistic form, achieving a most lifelike and down-to-earth effect in the representation of his figures. Other characteristic icons by Ushakov are his "Archangel Michael" and his "Mother of God" (both in the Tretyakov Gallery). The distinctive feature of Ushakov's "Trinity", and also of his icon "The Lord's Supper", is his attempt to obtain a lifelike effect by the use of linear perspective, thus breaking away from the long established tradition of representation in a single plane and at the same time bringing out the concrete reality of the event depicted.

It must be admitted that Ushakov's "Trinity" lacks the harmony and profound philosophical significance of Andrey Rublëv's icon on the same subject. The attempt to achieve vivid realism in the representation of the scene has to some extent overshadowed the revelation of the deeper recesses of the human mind and spirit. Moreover the weakness of Ushakov's work lay in the poverty and monotony of its colouring.

The saints depicted in Ushakov's icons are immeasurably nearer ordinary human beings than those in earlier icons. Their faces are painted in bright colours, the volumes are conveyed by the use of light and shade, and the hair is rendered with a smooth wash. The figures are remarkable for their naturalness: a characteristic which was entirely new and represented a daring and stimulating departure from the conventional style imposed by tradition. As an example of Ushakov's work, and one which illustrates the originality of his approach, we may take "The Tree of the Russian Kingdom" (Tretyakov Gallery), an allegorical composition representing the establishment of the kingdom by Ivan Kalita and the Metropolitan Peter, who are shown planting a tree which stands for Russia. The representations of the Kremlin and the Cathedral of the Dormition, and even more strikingly the portraits of Tsar Aleksey Mikhaylovich and Tsarina Mariya, show a powerful sense of realism. In this work exact portraiture was combined with allegorical significance, which itself had a precise historical reference and was immediately comprehensible to the observer. This concern with portraiture was characteristic of all Ushakov's work; and we know from the written sources that he painted portraits on canvas of Tsars Aleksey Mikhaylovich and Fëdor Alekseevich.

In his engraving of "The Seven Deadly Sins" Uskakov shows great skill in depicting the various attitudes and expressions of the naked human body. There are a number of other engravings based on drawings by him.

The 17th century saw the development of a new genre of painting in Russia, the *parsuna* (from the Latin *persona*) or representation of an ordinary human being. This was not yet a portrait in the modern sense — the *parsuna* lay somewhere between a realistic portrait and an icon — but it was an original and distinctive work of art in its own right. There was an active school of *parsuna*-painting not only in Russia but in the Ukraine.

The icon-painters now developed a characteristic manner in which, while many of the techniques of icon-painting were preserved, the figures were no longer abstract but wholly concrete, representing distinctive personalities and real human beings. As a rule the *parsuna* was painted on a wooden panel, though examples on canvas are also found. The artist's technique was almost exactly the same as with an icon. He hollowed out a cavity on the surface of the panel, the "shrine", covered this with a ground coat, sketched out his design and then laid on the colours. These works preserved not only the formal characteristics of icon-painting but the same artistic vision, the same conceptions of perspective, of space and of colouring. The figures were rigid, represented in a single plane, with no facial expression. The artists showed great interest in the representation of ornament, and frequently also in the inscriptions giving the names of the characters or other explanatory material.

But although the techniques used were those of icon-painting the figures represented were no longer abstract personages but real living people. The artists aimed at a faithful rendering of their distinctive individual characteristics, and the shapes of the heads, the faces, the figures and the garments were all taken from life. And yet, although the people depicted in these works are recognisable individuals, they are still caught up in the rigidity and conventionality of icon-painting and have not yet come to life.

The *parsuna* had long existed as a genre in Russian art, but the period of its greatest flowering came in the 17th century. Paul of Aleppo, describing the tombs in the Archangel Cathedral in Moscow in 1655, records that "above each tomb is a figure of the occupant as he was in life." Vladimirov also speaks in his *Treatise* of the necessity of achieving a faithful representation of the human figure in the *parsuna*, and many of the artists of this period painted from life. The interest shown in the *parsuna* was in fact merely one aspect of the contemporary concern with human personality.

In our eyes the *parsuna* has many archaic features, but to the men of that day it was a new form of art, an entirely novel type of artistic creation which was closely related to everyday life and reality.

Outstanding examples of the 17th century *parsuna* are the portraits of Tsar Aleksey Mikhaylovich Romanov, shown holding the orb and sceptre of royalty, and his son Tsar Fëdor Alekseevich (both in the Historical Museum in Moscow). Another characteristic example which illustrates all the distinctive features of the genre is a portrait of Prince M.V. Skopin-Shuysky (Tretyakov Gallery) *(Plate p. 59)*, a prominent 17th century statesman and a successful military commander who freed many Russian towns from foreign occupation and later died by poison, administered by his enemies. His dark green kaftan is covered with gold and silver brocade and richly adorned with pearls and precious stones. The round face, the high forehead, the bold upward curve of the eyebrows and the small round eyes make this the portrait of a distinctive and recognisable individual. At the top of the picture are an inscription and a representation of the "Saviour not Made with Hands". The rigidity of pose and the manner of rendering the ornament are still very characteristic of the icon-painting tradition; but at the same time we are struck by the genuine individuality shown in the portrayal of the sitter.

Another typical *parsuna* is a large canvas by an unknown artist representing the nobleman V.F. Lyutkin (1698, Historical Museum). This is not merely a small head-and-shoulders figure, but a large-scale formal portrait. Lyutkin is shown at full length and in life size, against the background of a red velvet curtain. Here again, however, the figure is represented in a single plane and in accordance with the accepted conventions; and — again following the traditions of icon-painting — there is no sense of space.

It was this genre, however, which gave rise to the realistic portrait, later to play such a prominent part in the history of Russian art. The *parsuna* represented a transitional stage between the icon and the portrait, which was by no means an 18th century invention but had a considerable pedigree of its own.

The graphic art of the 17th century shows many new features. It was a period of intensive development of the various genres, and of a steady increase in significance. Like 17th century painting, the graphic art of the period showed a constant interest in new methods and new ideas.

The records have preserved the names of a large number of engravers and draughtsmen who worked in the Pechatny Dvor, the Moscow printing-house, during this period, including such leading artists of the day as Ushakov, Zubov and Chirin.

In the first half of the century the art of the woodcut rose to importance. It was practised both in Moscow and in other towns, particularly in monasteries, and was used to illustrate books of both religious and secular character. Particularly fine examples of the graphic art of this period are the woodcuts by Kondraty Ivanov in a *Gospel* published in 1627, which is remarkable not only for its fine portraits of the Evangelists but for the beautifully executed decorations in which each page is framed. Of great interest also are the woodcuts in an *Alphabet* of 1637, which illustrate the text with a variety of scenes from everyday life, including a number of genre subjects.

In these works we are struck by the artists' skill in tracing their delicate patterns on wood, by the virtuosity with which they are able to render ornamental scrollwork, architectural detail and the human figure. In later years the traditions of wood-engraving were to be perpetuated in folk art, in popular prints and broadsheets *(lubki)*.

In the second half of the century the woodcut gave place to the new technique of engraving on metal, which represented an advance in refinement. An early, but already entirely professional, example of engraving on copper is Simon Ushakov's print of "The Seven Deadly Sins", in drypoint technique; and the same artist was responsible for other engravings which appeared in books of the period. Another outstanding master of the art of engraving was Afanasy Trukhmensky, who produced many fine prints.

Seventeenth century engraving is a rich and productive field which has close connections with the work being done in other genres at this time. It has not yet, however, received the thorough study which it undoubtedly requires.

Russian sculpture can look back on a long history, the origins of which are lost in the mists of time; and the early masters of plastic art, like artists working in other genres, created works which expressed the great aesthetic ideals of the period.

Throughout the whole course of its development Russian sculpture was intimately connected with folk art, and this gave it a distinctive national identity and a characteristic beauty of its own.

The works of ancient Russian plastic art which have come down to us attest the considerable development of this genre and the prominent place which sculpture occupied in the life of the people. Many of the works which have survived are reliefs depicting a variety of allegorical scenes, or sometimes

merely vegetable or geometric ornament. Of particular quality are the ornamental motifs, which show an exuberant imagination, an interest in decorative patterns and a shrewd appreciation of the possibilities of the medium.

Although the use of sculpture in churches was frowned on by the ecclesiastical authorities, it nevertheless contrived to make a considerable place for itself in the form of reliefs, carved ornament, the framework of iconostases and the *oklady* (masking frames) of the numerous icons. In all this work religious themes alternate with secular subjects, contemporary motifs with old pagan ones, and carving by skilled professional artists with work in the folk tradition, producing a diversity of pattern which gives it an unmistakable identity of its own.

The favourite material of the early Russian sculptors was wood. The passage of time, however, inevitably erodes the substance of the wood, blurs the sharp outlines of the carving, smoothes down the contrasts and destroys the colouring. It is a short-lived material which does not stand up to the ravages of the centuries. Nevertheless the few examples of wood carving that have survived are sufficient to indicate the remarkable beauty and the infinite variety of form which it achieved in its day.

Much of this work was of a religious character, and most of it was intended for the embellishment of churches. In spite of this it was not wholly confined within the requirements of ecclesiastical dogma; for the craftsmen whose carvings decorated the churches of the day were concerned to express their own conception of reality.

The carved decoration of the iconostases of the period — either sculpture in the round or carving in low relief — is remarkable for its elegance, its rich beauty and its exuberant imagination. A riot of carved garlands soars upwards in an intricate and fanciful pattern; the paintings are framed in splendid carved ornament, gilded or painted; and the surface of the iconostasis may be enriched with wooden figures of saints or cupids, adding to the total effect with a rich interplay of light and shade.

This carved ornament was a characteristic and essential element of the iconostases of the period: it was part of the very structure of the iconostasis and not merely a frame for the painting, adding an element of plastic beauty which enhanced the total effect. The decorative possibilities of carving were fully realised, and were exploited with great skill to create elegant church interiors. Although in the early part of the century the decoration of the iconostasis retained the flatness of the previous period, the pattern changed in the second half of the century. The carved decorations became much more three-dimensional and more complex in design; carving in high relief, and sometimes fully in the round, became increasingly common. In some churches, indeed, the icons and the painting are no longer the central feature but take second place to the richly carved ornament of the iconostasis.

As a rule the iconostases were decorated with complex patterns of vegetable ornament — including fruit, elaborate garlands and flowers — which varied widely from church to church. The carving was usually covered with gilding. Through all its diversity of design, however, the ornament of the iconostases had to fit in with certain structural requirements. The vertical colonnettes, which were often twisted, emphasised the soaring upward movement of the screen, and the position of the doors was marked by a semicircular arch.

Good examples of the use of carving to decorate church interiors are provided by the "royal doors" from a church in the village of Vozdvizhenskoe, near Zagorsk, and the Church of St John the Forerunner in Tolchkovo. In these buildings the carving has become an end in itself. Carved ornament of extraordinary richness is also found in the royal doors from the Church of St Nicholas of the Great Cross (now in the refectory church in the Monastery of the Trinity and St Sergius) *(Plate p. 62)*, the iconostasis in the Church of the Dormition in Pokrovka, and the iconostasis in the Church of the Sign in Dubrovitsi.

In the 17th century wood continued to be the sculptor's main material, being used on a large scale not only in churches but in ordinary secular building. The mansions of prosperous citizens were richly decorated with sculpture and with carved surrounds to the doors, windows and balconies. Carving was also much used for interior decoration. According to contemporary accounts the carved ornament of the old timber palace in the village of Kolomenskoe was of particular splendour, being known as "the eighth wonder of the world".

The skill of the carvers was also applied to the decoration of various articles of domestic use. Chairs, tables, cupboard doors and the lids of wooden chests were covered with intricate ornament, often based on vegetable motifs and incorporating birds and animals, all ingeniously combined into an intricate and homogeneous pattern.

The evolution of sculpture in the round during the 17th century shows the same general processes at work as in painting. The representations of Christ and of the saints become much more three-dimensional and realistic and stress the individual characteristics of the figures. Typical examples of this are figures of a hermit (Russian Museum) and St Parasceve or St Pyatnitsa (Perm Museum) *(Plate p. 62)*. Although still maintaining the static pose and the constraint of the traditional style, they are nevertheless remarkable for their realism and human individuality. Wood sculpture was almost always painted in bright colours, giving it an immediate appeal.

In the sculpture of the 17th century we also meet some of the favourite figures of Russian tradition, treated by different artists in their varying ways — in particular St George the Victorious, St Nikita the Warrior and St Nicholas of Mozhaysk.

The Museum in Perm contains a collection of material which is of particular importance to students of the history of sculpture in wood. This shows the usual traditional features, with a distinctive local tinge which enhances their expressiveness and effect.

As a characteristic example of 17th century plastic art we may consider a magnificent figure of the Tsarevich Dmitry on a silver reliquary from the Archangel Cathedral in Moscow, carved in 1630 by Gavrila Ovdokimov *(Plate p. 61)*. The figure of Dmitry is treated three-dimensionally. He is shown against a richly decorated background, wearing a splendid garment adorned with precious stones, the ornament on which combines with the background to form a unified pattern. The expression on the Tsarevich's face, his rather broad cheekbones and his staring eyes are accurately rendered, but at the same time the artist has managed to convey the youthfulness and naturalness of the boy's face. Another work showing similar characteristics is the figure of Aleksandr Svirsky (1643, Russian Museum), which is also carved on the cover of a reliquary.

The sculpture of the 17th century includes many representations of animals and birds, and in particular of lions — the symbol of power — which were used in the most varied decorative contexts. Whether curled up in a ball or stretched out at full length, these lions are always full of expressiveness; often they are distorted with great virtuosity into a geometrical pattern and perform an almost purely ornamental function.

Elements of plastic ornament were also widely used in applied art, on a variety of dishes and vessels, on silver cups and goblets, on articles of church furnishing, and so on.

Thus the sculpture of the 17th century not only developed with remarkable vigour but evolved many characteristics that were entirely new. As in the field of painting, realistic elements became predominant, while sculpture in the round gradually superseded the conventional low relief of earlier years and the representation of the human figure played an increasingly important part.

Applied art also made rapid progress during the 17th century. Although much work of this kind was destroyed or plundered during the Time of Troubles at the beginning of the century, the various crafts developed with renewed vigour in the following period, and the losses of earlier years were largely made good. The goldsmiths' and silversmiths' workshops in Moscow were kept busily employed producing jewellery, for which there was an enormous demand, stimulated by the ostentatious luxury of the court and the feudal nobility.

Much artistic effort was also devoted to the decoration of various articles of domestic use. Dishes, combs, cups and other objects produced by the craftsmen of this period were often real works of art. Bone-carving and glass production also developed on a considerable scale. The chief centre for the production of such objects was again the Kremlin Armoury.

The technique of engraving metal, particularly silver, now came into use. Some cups dating from this period, on which the ornament is usually left bare but the ground is covered with niello, are of striking and individual beauty.

These works of applied art show great variety of technique and design; and work of high quality was produced by various local schools, each with its own distinctive characteristics.

Many works of folk art also have a particular charm. Wooden vessels of various kinds, embroidery, furniture and decorative painting played a considerable part in the life of the 17th century, providing evidence of the lively imagination and the eternal quest for beauty which was so abundantly expressed in the artistic creation of ordinary people.

Equally remarkable are the various articles forged from metal — locks, hinges, doors, objects of everyday use, ornaments. In this period craftsmen did not merely produce articles of this kind for their own use but also manufactured them for sale. The local markets of Russia were now united to form a single market, and this facilitated a wide distribution of the output of local craftsmen.

An important branch of applied art was the production of *oklady* (frames) for icons and liturgical books. The exquisitely delicate ornament, the richness and variety of the relief, and the precious stones with which they were inlaid contributed to make these *oklady* works of the highest artistic quality. The edges of the frames sometimes contained a number of separate panels or medallions depicting a variety of different themes.

At the end of the century the technique of enamelling appeared, and rapidly achieved great popularity.

The many objects of applied art dating from this period which can be seen in the Kremlin Armoury, including some treasures from the collections of Princes and Tsars, make an immediate appeal to the visitor's imagination and convey some impression not only of the prodigal luxury of the Russian court but also of the exquisite skill of Russian craftsmen, their vigorous creative imagination and the remarkable folk traditions to which they gave expression.

The art of the 17th century represents the culmination of the development of the older Russian art. We can see it today as a period of splendid achievement which crowned the history of mediaeval Russian culture. Seventeenth century art did not in any sense mark a decline or an anticlimax: it had great qualities of its own and showed a spirit of innovation which produced a rich harvest of aesthetic achievement.

At the end of the 17th century a great stratum of the native culture of Russia passed into history. The start of the new century was a turning point, a frontier between the old and the new; and there is perhaps no more significant frontier in the whole course of Russian history. But this does not mean that the art of the older Russia disappeared without trace. The traditions of the 17th century proved remarkably persistent and played an important part in the culture of the following period. The new and forward-looking elements in Russian art were cherished and carefully preserved into our own day, while the outdated and reactionary elements were swept away during the turmoil of the 18th century.

II   THE EIGHTEENTH CENTURY
A PERIOD OF NEW DISCOVERIES

The 18th century is a period of great significance in Russian history: "an age of intelligence and an age of extravagance", an age of great discoveries, of astonishing scientific advance, of far-reaching transformations in the structure of the Russian state.

During this period Russia developed from a backward country of which western Europe knew little into a rich and powerful nation of steadily increasing authority. It was in this period, too, that the country cast off the fetters of the Middle Ages and the human mind was able to pursue in unrestrained freedom its quest for understanding of the laws which governed the natural world. "Unforgettable century, which to delighted mortals grants truth, freedom and light!" wrote Aleksandr Radishchev. And yet it was also a period of savage repression which saw the triumph of serfdom, the enslavement of the peasants and the reduction of the mass of the people to hopeless pauperism.

The 18th century saw not only a mighty upsurge of the social consciousness of the Russian people and a great advance in social and philosophical thinking, but also a rich flowering of art. The great names of Russian science and literature — Lomonosov, Fonvizin, Radishchev, Derzhavin and Novikov — are matched by those of artists like Shubin and Rokotov, Levitsky and Bazhenov, Kozlovsky and Losenko, whose work gave expression to many of the fundamental ideas of the century and enriched the heritage of Russian culture.

In spite of its long history Russian art was still a young art, engaged in a process of intensive development, advancing to fresh achievement in reaction against older ideas, and eagerly assimilating new ideas which had hitherto been beyond its compass. Its growth during this period was remarkable:

new genres were created and developed, new themes were treated, new standards of artistic form were achieved.

This development received a powerful stimulus at the beginning of the century, during the reign of Peter the Great, when Russian art, reacting against the influence of the outmoded mediaeval culture, established itself as a secular and realistic art, fully responsive to the needs of contemporary life. This was not, however, achieved without difficulty, for throughout the century the representatives of the new trend found themselves in perpetual conflict with those who still clung to the older ideas.

In recent years the study of 18th century Russian art has advanced rapidly. The work of the artists

of this period has been collected and recorded, carefully studied and restored; and this has greatly enlarged our knowledge of its development and has contributed to the great reputation which it now enjoys.

In spite of the substantial progress which its industry and trade had made in the 17th century Russia was still far behind the more advanced nations of western Europe. The country's greatest handicap was its unnatural isolation, its lack of any access to the sea, which was a major obstacle to the development of trade. Progress could be made only by resolute measures designed to achieve a complete transformation.

Then came the "Northern War" against the Swedes, which lasted twenty-one years but finally ended in victory and in the liberation of Russian territory and the opening up of the Gulf of Finland. Russia had now gained an outlet to the sea and had become a great maritime power.

During Peter's reign Russian industry made rapid progress, a powerful fleet was built and a national army created. Science and learning advanced as never before, the output of the printing presses increased, and the first Russian newspaper appeared. New educational institutions were established and a reform of the administrative machinery carried out, with the creation of the Senate and the twelve administrative "Colleges". Peter made the Church subordinate to the State and established the Synod to manage ecclesiastical affairs. The Petrine period was a time of great changes in Russia — changes in the national way of life, in manners and in dress. It was not surprising, therefore, that Russian art also underwent a change.

Peter the Great's achievement was to deliver Russia from its condition of mediaeval backwardness and make it one of the most powerful nations in Europe. In this process all that was obsolete and outdated was rejected, and the new elements which matched the spirit of the age received the encouragement and support which enabled them to develop. Mediaeval Russia was now finally relegated to

limbo. Not unexpectedly, the administrative changes introduced at the beginning of the century encountered many difficulties and much opposition. The result was a bitter conflict in which victory was bound to go to the shrewdest of the contestants, the man who knew his objective and set out boldly to achieve it; and Peter's success in carrying through his plans made him one of the most popular European statesmen of the day.

Unfortunately a number of works published in Europe and America have been concerned to propagate the idea that Russian art in this period was dependent on foreign art, that it lost its national characteristics at the turn of the 17th and 18th centuries. This is not a new theory, but has been current for something over a hundred years. As early as the beginning of the 19th century the Slavophils, in denying the legitimacy and historical appropriateness of the changes carried out by Peter, were led to reject also the new school of art, which they regarded as imitative and alien to the national culture of Russia. This was also the view of some later critics. Towards the end of the 19th century and in the early years of the 20th it was unequivocally expressed by the Russian art historians N. Vrangel and A. Benois. Thus

Vrangel refers in one of his works to the "two centuries of confusion and disorder in the cultural life of Russia" which began in the early years of the 18th century. In his view Peter the Great had done Russia a disservice in forcibly injecting alien standards of artistic style, and Russian art was an "artificial amalgam" created by foreigners. The same point of view, expressed in different words, can still be heard in our own day.

Soviet art historians have long since demonstrated the error of such views. A careful study of the material now available has made it possible to reach a clearer understanding

of the history of 18th century Russian art; and this has not only enlarged our knowledge of its development but has enabled us to study its relationship with the art of other countries and has illuminated the process of emergence of the new secular and realistic art. The Russian realism of the 18th century was not an importation from the West, nor the result of imitating Western fashions, but was a natural and profoundly national phenomenon with a long-established and extremely fruitful tradition rooted in the past. Russian realism resembles the corresponding foreign schools in the same way as French art resembles Italian or German; but these resemblances do not in any way obscure the special characteristics or the distinctive national identity of the different schools.

Those who argue against the independence of Russian art usually make great play with the country's active links with the West in the 18th century and the large number of foreign artists who worked in Russia. These facts are not in dispute, but they by no means lead to the conclusion which is drawn from them.

Peter the Great did in fact offer a ready welcome to foreigners, since he was anxious to benefit from their experience in the various fields of science and culture. The assimilation of this foreign experience was one of the prime objectives of this period, for it would have been folly to leave Russia to pursue a course of slow and gradual evolution, taking no account of the progress already made in the West. At the very beginning of the century several hundred foreign specialists came to Russia; and later, after the introduction of a law giving them special privileges and freedom of worship, their number was substantially increased. Among them were artists like the engraver Adrian Schönebeck and the

sculptor Konrad Osner; later came the painters Louis Caravacque, Gottfried Danhauer and Georg Gsell and the sculptor Carlo Rastrelli.

These foreigners came to Russia on contract for three years, and usually then returned to their own country. Some of them, however, stayed in Russia and came to regard it as a second home. The great majority remained faithful to their native style of art and played no part in the development of Russian art. Only one or two of these incomers showed a real awareness of the requirements of Russian society, set themselves new aesthetic objectives, and created works which can properly be considered as belonging to the history of Russian art.

Peter, anxious that his country should profit from the achievements of foreign artists, sent young men into other countries, enjoining them to concern themselves with whatever might be of use to Russia. It is significant that not one of the Russian artists whose stay abroad was financed in this way became a mere mechanical imitator. They learned the secrets of their craft, the principles of realistic draughtsmanship and the laws of anatomy, studied the heritage of the old masters and familiarised themselves with the work of their contemporaries; but all of them preserved their national individuality, so that their work can be distinguished at once from that of a foreign artist. The same method of assisting young artists to travel abroad was employed in other European countries at this period, with no less fruitful results.

Peter the Great's active concern with the development of art was dictated by his recognition of its vital importance. Thus the circumstances of Russian life in this period favoured the development of book production, and Peter sought to promote this craft by every possible means. "We cannot do without the artist and the engraver," he wrote, recognising the importance of providing illustrations for the literature which was now being published. For this purpose there was associated with the St Petersburg printing-house a special school for the training of artist illustrators. During Peter's reign a project was put forward for the establishment of an Academy of Arts, to provide proper professional training — "without which," the proposal suggested, "artists cannot have a sufficient grounding in their crafts." Unfortunately Peter's untimely death delayed the realisation of this plan by thirty years.

The new ideas of the day were reflected in an impressive flowering of architecture. Never before had there been such intense building activity in Russia as in the early years of the 18th century. The building industry was reorganised to enable it to meet the new demands. New factories were established for the production of building materials, a standard size of brick was introduced, and general directives were issued on the design and construction of buildings. New types of structure appeared for the first time in Russia, in a vast programme of building and civil engineering work which included shipyards, works of fortification, factories, canals and locks, museums, administrative buildings and much else besides.

The new tasks which now faced the architectural profession underlined the need to train architects of wide competence capable of dealing with commissions of considerable scale and complexity. Books were published on the theory of architecture, special schools were established, and students were sent abroad at State expense. The first students sent abroad in this way during Peter's reign were Ivan Korobov, Pëtr Eropkin, Ivan Mordvinov and Ivan Michurin, who were subsequently responsible for much building work and made important contributions to the history of Russian architecture.

The first buildings of the 18th century were erected in Moscow, and showed the features which were to be typical of later Russian architecture. These buildings were the Menshikov Palace (also known as the Lefort Palace), built in 1707-08, and the Arsenal

in the Moscow Kremlin (1702-06), with its splendid entrance designed by D. Ivanov and M. Choglokov.

The most important and characteristic building erected in Moscow in the early years of the century was the Menshikov Tower (1704-07), designed by the gifted architect and sculptor Ivan Zarudny. This church, cruciform in plan and richly embellished with carved ornament, was originally crowned with a spire and bore a strong resemblance to the "tent"-roofed churches of the 17th century; it was also the undoubted prototype of the Cathedral of SS. Peter and Paul in St Petersburg. The scrolls on either side of the entrance, the pilasters and the series of superimposed openwork octagons combined to give the building an air of lightness and elegance. Unfortunately a fire in the year 1723 destroyed the graceful spire and radically altered the appearance of the church. Zarudny was responsible for many other buildings in the city, including a triumphal gateway, a hospital, churches and houses. He was the leading Moscow architect of the early part of the century.

The Church of the Virgin of the Sign at Dubrovitsi, one of the masterpieces of Moscow architecture of the end of the 17th century and the early years of the 18th, is also attributed to Zarudny. Its very individual plan, its profusion of carved ornament and its octagonal tower finished with an iron coronet are very reminiscent of the baroque architecture of the architect's native Ukraine.

Thus in the early years of the 18th century there was intense building activity in Moscow, and its architecture, based though it was on the traditions of the previous century, began to develop a style characteristic of the new age. But this was only the beginning of the process: for the fullest and finest development of Petrine architecture we must look to the new capital of Russia, St Petersburg.

The establishment of a new capital city on the banks of the Neva, the transfer of the administrative centre of the country to a situation where it would be nearer the other countries of Europe, was an act of extreme boldness justified by a grandiose conception of policy. The new capital was intended to be an important military, commercial and cultural centre: it was to be Russia's "window on Europe".

The city was founded in May 1703, with the establishment of the fortress to which the name of St Petersburg was given; and in 1712 it was officially declared the capital of Russia. As the surrounding territory was recovered from the Swedes the city grew enormously and soon developed into a homogeneous community of an entirely new pattern, very different from the older Russian towns. It was laid out on a unified plan, largely determined by the course of the Neva and centred on the fortress. The new capital was built in stone, in sharp contrast to Moscow with its few stone churches lost in a sea of timber houses. Since there was no stone in the St Petersburg area, a decree was issued requiring all who entered the city to bring "three stones in each cart-load" as a contribution to the building of the capital. Soon a special Building Department was established to be responsible for the construction of the city. The streets were laid out on geometrically straight alignments, giving St Petersburg a very different aspect from the older Russian cities founded in the Middle Ages. From the beginning, too, standard house plans were laid down for citizens of different degrees of wealth and

social position; all of them, however, being relatively unpretentious and differing only in size.

As an example of the rationally planned architecture of this period we may take Peter's own Summer Palace, still to be seen in the Summer Garden. It is a relatively small building showing extreme restraint in the use of decoration, somewhat reminiscent of the residences of Dutch burghers. Peter had a particular liking for Dutch architecture, being impressed with its simple and functional style. Moreover the experience of Dutch builders seemed likely to be of particular value to St Petersburg in view of the similarity of the geographical conditions; for the abundance of water and the marshy ground on the banks of the Neva gave the surroundings of St Petersburg some similarity with the landscape of Holland. The buildings erected in the new capital in the early years of the century, however, had a distinctively Russian character, with only a very remote resemblance to Dutch architecture.

The builders of St Petersburg were faced with some unusually complex problems. The draining of the marshes, the improvement of the river banks, the procurement and transport of timber and stone, and finally the erection of the buildings and the laying out of the streets cost many thousands of human lives. In spite of all difficulties, however, the town was built in a remarkably short space of time and became one of the handsomest cities in the world.

The foundation of St Petersburg provided a powerful stimulus to the development of Russian art, since the city offered hundreds of skilled architects, sculptors, painters and other artists full scope for the exercise of their talents. The first buildings erected in the new capital were the Fortress and the Cathedral of SS. Peter and Paul. These were originally built in timber, but were later reconstructed in stone. They were designed by Domenico Tressini (c. 1670-1734), a native of Italy who settled in Russia and spent thirty years of his life there.

The fortress and the cathedral became the real centre of the city *(Plate p. 72)*. The extensive circuit of walls, with massive bastions projecting towards the river, had a menacing and formidable aspect which bore witness to the might of Russia. The structure of the fortress was remarkable for its homogeneity, and the architecture, while wholly functional, succeeded at the same time in achieving elegance and magnificence. This is particularly well exemplified by the famous Petrovsky Gate (1717-18), also designed by Tressini and decorated with carving by Konrad Osner *(Plate p. 75)*. Its distinctive baroque character is based on a strict conception of architectural function combined with the rational use of plastic ornament. The gate is a feature of notable elegance, while the fortress itself is an austere and ascetic structure; and it is precisely in this contrast that the architect seeks his effect.

The fortress is dominated by the Cathedral of SS. Peter and Paul, which with its massive tower and tall spire is one of the outstanding landmarks of the city *(Plate p. 73)*. It is true that the exterior — in a style rather reminiscent of the Menshikov Tower — is not particularly impressive; the interior, however, is magnificent. The most important feature of the building is the bell-tower, a three-storied structure which is drawn into a unified whole by the volutes on the angles and is crowned by the soaring spire with its figure of an angel. The spire can be seen from a great distance, and adds a distinctive note to the skyline of the city *(Plate p. 74)*.

The iconostasis in the Cathedral, carved by Ivan Zarudny, is a magnificent and very typical example of Petrine architecture. The richness of the modelling and the profusion of carved figures combine with the painted icons and the brightly coloured paintings under the dome to create an effect of great elegance and splendour. The pictures in the Cathedral were mostly painted by Russian artists.

Tressini's most important work, after the Cathedral of SS. Peter and Paul, was the Twelve Colleges in St Petersburg (now the State University), erected between 1721 and 1733 to house the various administrative departments of government. This was a long range of offices lying at right angles to the Neva, designed as a unified whole but with the separate sections distinguished by individual façades with pilasters and a small pediment, and with independent roofs. During the early years of the cen-

tury, too, building was carried out along the Neva embankments. Near the Twelve Colleges was built the Kunstkammer designed by Georg Johann Mattarnovi and Mikhail Zemtsov, with a characteristic octagonal tower linking the two lateral wings of the building. On the same embankment, a little downstream, was the Menshikov Palace designed by G.M. Fontana and Gottfried Schädel, a small building with projecting wings and pavilions, decorated with pilasters and a small semicircular pediment. As was normal with buildings along the river front, there was a small landing-stage in front of the palace, and behind it were various appurtenances, including a pleasure-garden, a kitchen-garden and domestic offices.

During the 1720s and 1730s the architects principally engaged in the building of St Petersburg were Korobov, Zemtsov and Eropkin. Zemtsov was responsible for laying out the Summer Garden and for building the "Halls of Ceremony" in the Garden, as well as for designing St Isaac's Church and the Anichkov Palace. Eropkin's name is associated with large-scale town development operations in St Petersburg.

Meanwhile the Admiralty dockyard was built on the left bank of the Neva and became the central point of an important district of the new city. From this point radiated three main thoroughfares: the Nevsky Prospekt — the principal street of the city — Gorokhovy Street and Voznesensky Street. The building of these streets substantially enlarged the scale of the city. At first the Admiralty had all the appearance of a fortress. It was surrounded on three sides by ramparts and a moat, and the angles

facing on to the Neva were reinforced by bastions from which cannon could command the river. Even in later years, when the danger of attack had disappeared, the building did not lose its fortress-like appearance, retaining its defences until the early years of the 19th century.

The Admiralty buildings were laid out in the form of the Greek letter п, with the open end facing the Neva, and consisted of a long range of two-storey buildings containing workshops, stores, armouries, foundries and so on. Considerable changes were made in the 1730s, when the building was reconstructed to the plans of Ivan Korobov. At this stage the Admiralty acquired its famous tower with the spire crowned by a ship, forming a focal point at which the principal streets of the city met *(Plate p. 76)*.

The Admiralty remained in this form throughout the 18th century, and it was not until 1805 that Adrian Zakharov undertook a large-scale reconstruction of the building. At this period it took on more or less its present appearance *(Plate p. 77)*. The original Petrine building with the characteristic

high roof and the modest pilasters ornamenting the façade was transformed into a classical structure with four pillared porticoes and a profusion of sculpture and carving. The ramparts and bastions were swept away and the moat was replaced by a tree-lined avenue, so that the building was now thrown open to the citizens of St Petersburg. It had in fact long ceased to be a dockyard, and now housed the administrative headquarters of the Russian navy. Fortunately Zakharov appreciated the merit of Korobov's spire and preserved it in its entirety, merely framing it in a classical colonnade.

The buildings erected in St Petersburg in the early years of the century differ in many respects from the architecture of 17th century Moscow, but they also show traditional features. One obvious example of this is the Cathedral of SS. Peter and Paul, which has no parallels in western European architecture but shows close links with earlier Russian building.

From the early years of the 18th century the development of the city proceeded on an organised plan. Great stress was laid on the regular design of the façades, the decoration of which had to be fitted into the framework of the classical orders. The buildings were embellished with volutes, figured pediments and carving, but this decoration was kept within reasonable bounds: the ornament was always restrained so that it played its proper part in the total architectural effect.

The building activity of Peter's reign was not of course confined to Moscow and St Petersburg. Much building was also done in the provinces. At Taganrog, in the Urals and Altay, at Tula and Petrozavodsk, and at Kazan there were erected individual buildings and large architectural ensembles showing in greater or lesser degree the characteristics of the Petrine style, its soberly functional approach, its restrained decoration and its logical organisation of structure. Among the many magnificent parks and gardens which were laid out during the 18th century Peterhof (now called Petrodvorets), on the shores of the Gulf of Finland near Leningrad, is outstanding for its beauty and the plastic unity of its design. It was created in the early years of the century as the summer residence of Peter the Great, and from the outset amazed foreign visitors by its magnificence, which entirely belied the accepted ideas about the backwardness of Russia.

The park and the Great Palace, built in the baroque style by Bartolommeo Rastrelli, lay on higher ground, with cascades and fountains decorated with sculpture running down the slopes. In the lower park, which stretched down to the shores of the Gulf of Finland, were other fountains and pavilions *(Plates pp. 78, 79, 89)*.

Of particular interest is Peter's private palace of Monplaisir, a single-storey building with large windows and a high roof in the Dutch style. Here Peter lived, dealt with government business and received foreign envoys. From the palace there was a view of Kronstadt, the principal fortress in the Gulf of Finland and the key to St Petersburg. Peterhof was designed by Peter himself. His original drawings have been preserved, showing the main buildings and fountains. The most impressive part of the whole complex is, of course, the Great Palace and its cascade, from which a canal runs down to the Gulf, flanked by two lines of small fountains *(Plate p. 89)*.

With their powerful upward-soaring jets and their variety of design the fountains of Peterhof achieve a gay and striking effect. Their chief interest lies in their sculpture. Originally this was in lead, but at the end of the 18th century the earlier work was replaced by bronze statues by the Russian sculptors Prokofyev, Shchedrin, Shubin and Martos. The central feature was a figure of Samson rending open the lion's jaws — an allegory of the battle of Poltava, in which Russia had decisively defeated the Swedes. This group, by Mikhail Kozlovsky, was rightly considered a masterpiece of decorative sculpture. Seen through the spray of the fountains, with the sunlight glittering on the water, these gilded figures take on a special beauty of their own.

Peterhof was frequently the scene of elaborate court festivities, in the preparation of which many skilled artists were employed. Of particular splendour were the firework displays, which were mounted with great lavishness and made a powerful impression on all who saw them. An English visitor wrote that anyone wishing to describe them must "dip his pen in a sea of rainbow-coloured ink."

ꙖКОВЪ · ТꙊРГЄНЄВЪ ⁖

Side by side with the construction of houses and public buildings and the laying out of parks, the old religious architecture in timber continued to develop during the early years of the 18th century. Of the considerable number of such buildings erected in this period perhaps the most fabulously beautiful as well as the most strikingly individual was the Church of the Transfiguration at Kizhi on Lake Onega, built in 1714 *(Plates pp. 86-87)*. This is a remarkable demonstration of the virtuosity and individuality of Russian architects, their soaring imagination and magnificent technical mastery. The church, built on the very shores of the lake, standing 120 feet high and embellished with twenty-two domes, makes an unforgettable impression on the visitor. A variety of legends and traditions grew up round this building, which was reputed far and wide as a marvel of architectural skill; and it is easy to see why.

The timber domes are arranged in a pyramidal pattern, in a soaring upward movement which gives the church its special beauty and picturesqueness. The uniqueness of its proportions and silhouette, the masterly organisation of volumes and the delicacy of the carving combine to demonstrate the superb skill of the builders. The church was constructed without a single nail; and it is said that when the architect, Master Nester, had completed his task he flung his axe into the waters of the lake, with the words: "There has never been, is not, and never shall be such another!" And we are compelled to admit the truth of this claim.

The period of Peter the Great was notable for its concern with human personality, its belief in the limitless possibilities open to man; and this eager interest in man produced a vigorous and fruitful development of portrait-painting, as well as influencing the whole course of development of Russian art.

A factor of fundamental importance in this connection was the great interest taken in Russia from the beginning of the 18th century onwards in the study of the physical world. This interest was a very characteristic feature of the period. Russian science made great strides, an Academy of Science was founded, new schools were established, book production expanded. The study of nature and the effort to understand the inner meaning of the processes which men saw at work in the world around them were foremost among the preoccupations of the age; and this inevitably had its effect on the art of the period and promoted the development of the principles of realism.

The art of icon-painting, governed by mediaeval conceptions of human life and the function of art, was no longer adequate in the 18th century to express the strivings of the new age and give substance to the contemporary aesthetic ideal. The realities of life, in all their variety and infinite complexity, presented the artist with new problems and required new forms and techniques for their expression. The artists of the 18th century had not merely to learn to draw and paint in a different way, but to see and interpret differently a whole world of real and not merely abstract values. On the other hand the older ideas which had grown up in the course of the centuries had become part of the very substance of art, had acquired an immensely rich tradition, and were taken for granted through sheer force of habit. It was inevitable, therefore, that the development of the new secular and realistic art should give rise to the bitterest controversy.

Icon painting did not die out in the 18th century. Considerable numbers of icons were painted in this period, many churches were decorated with painting, and the traditions of the genre were preserved. But inevitably the new secular and realistic art had an effect on the character of religious painting, influencing both its subject matter and its artistic form.

The characteristics of the new style were shown most clearly in the field of portrait painting. From the early years of the century we have the series of portraits of the "Unholy Synod" — the name Peter jokingly gave to the boon companions of his leisure hours, in ironical allusion to the Holy Synod which governed the Church. These portraits bear all the marks of a period of transition. They are still strongly imbued with the influence of the *parsuna*, although in many respects they show similarities with the realistic portrait which was to become so popular in the 18th century. The figures are still represented in a single plane, although the individual likeness of the sitter is now much more clearly expressed than in the *parsuna*. The artist still tends to include the traditional ornament, and sometimes there is an inscription attached to the portrait. Typical examples are the portraits of Vasikov, Count Apraksin and Yakov Turgenev *(Plate p. 94)*. The best of the series is the portrait of Turgenev, whose face is presented with great realism, though the pose still shows a certain rigidity.

This series of portraits is of great importance as an illustration of the direction in which painting was developing at the turn of the century, and can be seen as occupying a transitional position in the history of secular and realistic art.

The leading practitioners of the new style in the first part of the 18th century were Andrey Matveev (1710-39) and Ivan Nikitin (c. 1690-1741). Matveev was a scion of a noble family who found his way to St Petersburg as a young man. There his enthusiasm for painting brought him to Peter's notice, and his future career was decided. He was sent to Holland, where he spent some years perfecting his skill. Thereafter he returned to Russia and devoted himself to decorative painting, being responsible for the decoration of numerous buildings in St Petersburg, including in particular the Cathedral of SS. Peter and Paul. He also achieved fame as an unusually gifted portrait painter, a characteristic example of his work being his "Self-portrait with Wife".

Ivan Nikitin, the son of a Moscow priest, had a very different career, and one which ended in tragedy. In his youth, while a singer in a court choir, he also worked as a portrait painter, in which field he showed remarkable talent. Thereafter he spent some years in France and Italy. Even before going abroad Nikitin was well known to the Tsar, who was always ready to help and encourage any artists who showed particular gifts. Peter took pride in Nikitin's skill, and when the artist visited Danzig asked his wife Catherine, who was staying there at the time, to use her influence to secure him a commission for a portrait of the Polish king Augustus II — "so that it may be known," wrote Peter, "that we too have skilled craftsmen."

Returning to Russia in 1718, Nikitin acquired a considerable reputation and painted a long series of portraits of his contemporaries.

Nikitin's work has broken free from the influence of the *parsuna* and is remarkable for its fine draughtsmanship and accurate likenesses, as well as for its penetrating insight into the character of the sitter. As an example of these qualities we may take his portrait of Peter the Great (Russian Museum) *(Plate p. 96)*. Peter's portrait was painted by many artists, both Russian and foreign, who were usually

interested in the figure of the Emperor, the man who ruled over the destinies of a great Empire, the great military commander. He was therefore frequently represented wearing armour and a military cloak, or sometimes on horseback, clad in magnificent garments, against the background of a battle. The distinctive quality of Nikitin's portrait, on the other hand, is its profound humanity. Although the picture shows only Peter's head it conveys a powerful impression of his intelligence and humanity. Nikitin sees Peter as a thinking, suffering man, and this is what distinguishes his work from many other contemporary portraits of the Tsar.

Nikitin also painted a well-known portrait of "Peter the Great on his Deathbed" (also in the Russian Museum).

A painting which is generally regarded as one of his best works is his "Portrait of a Hetman" (Plate p. 97), evidently painted in the middle 1720s. This is a striking likeness of an elderly warrior who gazes sternly at the spectator, his furrowed brow and intent stare reflecting the hardships he has endured in the course of his service. It is a portrait of great psychological penetration which reveals the inmost being of the sitter.

The process of breaking free from the traditions of the past was inevitably accompanied by difficulties and conflicts, and in effect occupied the whole of the 18th century. The persistence with which some artists still clung to the old tradition of the *parsuna* is demonstrated in the work of Ivan Nikitin's brother Roman, who was still firmly attached to the traditional style. In spite of his obvious talent and technical proficiency he was still dominated by the ideas of the older school. This can be clearly seen in his portraits of members of the Stroganov family (Plate p. 95). With their rigidity of pose, their schematic draughtsmanship and their delight in ornament, these works seem extraordinarily old-fashioned in comparison with the profoundly realistic portraits painted by Ivan Nikitin.

After Peter's death there were many changes in Russia; and there were changes also in Ivan Nikitin's life. He was accused of opposition to the government, arrested, flogged, and sent to Siberia. Some years later he was pardoned; but the hardships he had undergone had sapped his strength and he died on the way back to St Petersburg.

The construction of the new capital gave a stimulus to the development of decorative painting, which was much in demand for the embellishment of the new palaces and public buildings. The novel features of this genre were its secular subject matter and its extensive use of allegorical themes, which were depicted with great concreteness and often reflected real historical events. Unfortunately little of the decorative painting of this period has been preserved, since most of the buildings have been destroyed; but we can gain an impression of its quality from the paintings in the palace of Monplaisir at Peterhof, in the Summer Palace and in the Kadriorg Palace in Tallinn.

The new pattern of life in Russia was reflected also in graphic art, which from the earliest years of the 18th century was in process of active development. Indeed it was perhaps this branch of art which first showed the effect of the new trends which were appearing in Russian culture. It developed in two directions — easel drawing and illustration. (We have already referred to Peter the Great's interest in the development of book production, which was closely bound up with the work of the engravers).

In the early days it was found necessary to reinforce the native Russian artists by bringing in a number of foreigners, the most important of whom were Adrian Schönebeck and Peter Pickaerdt. The former did not stay long in Russia, but Pickaerdt remained for over ten years.

An outstanding contribution to the art of engraving in Russia was made by Aleksey Zubov (1682 to after 1744), an artist trained in the Moscow Armoury, who produced a famous series of views of St Petersburg. These prints give us a faithful picture of the new capital, with its palaces, its wide avenues and parks, its network of canals and the bustling life of its streets. Apart from their purely documentary value Zubov's prints are highly competent works of considerable artistic merit.

Later, in the 1750s, a further series of engravings of St Petersburg was produced by another prominent artist engraver, Mikhail Makhaev (1716-70). In contrast to Zubov's disciplined draughtsmanship, his work was smoother and more picturesque, and he was more catholic in his choice of subjects than the artists of the early years of the century. He did not confine himself exclusively to the city of St Petersburg, but portrayed scenes in the suburban districts and in palaces and parks, as well as in Moscow.

In the early years of the 18th century there was also a remarkable growth of interest in sculpture. It is generally considered that the most flourishing branches of art in this period were architecture, graphic art and portrait painting; but sculpture by no means fell behind these other genres. The creation of the new capital, the erection of numerous palaces and public buildings, the laying out of parks and the interior decoration of the new houses all led to a demand for works of plastic art. It was at this period that the special qualities of sculpture and the great possibilities of the medium first began to be fully realised.

The early years of the century saw an increased interest in classical sculpture and an appreciation of the high degree of professional skill which it had achieved. Significantly, it was during these years that the splendid ancient marble figure of the Tauride Venus was acquired in Italy and brought to St Petersburg. It was installed in a specially constructed pavilion in the Summer Garden, and is now one of the treasures of the Hermitage. The developing interest in sculpture naturally turned men's thoughts towards Italy, both ancient and modern; and it was accordingly to Leghorn that a group of gifted young artists were sent to be trained in the art of sculpture.

The great importance of sculpture in the life of Russian society is demonstrated by the extensive use made of it in the decoration of Peterhof. Sculpture was also the principal form of decoration in the Summer Garden and the source of its exquisite beauty: and it similarly contributed to the charm of many other parks in and around St Petersburg, Moscow and other towns.

Sculpture was also used with great skill for the adornment of the new buildings erected in the cities of Russia. The rational simplicity of early 18th century architecture was enriched with plastic decoration, principally in the form of simple reliefs and mouldings, which harmonised perfectly with the clear-cut outlines of the façades, the curved volutes of the cornices and the capitals of the pilasters. In this period the whole aspect of the city, the lines of the façades and the pattern of streets and squares were conceived in plastic terms.

The wooden carving found in so many churches in northern Russia — including not only low relief but sculpture in the round — remained within the folk tradition. The works of these local craftsmen, who are for the most part nameless, are remarkable for their acute observation and perfection of skill. The collections of this sculpture in the museums of Vologda and Perm contain work of outstanding merit which has not yet been the subject of detailed study. These local sculptors have something of the monumental style of the icon-painters, combined with an acutely realistic vision of the world. And many other museums in Russia also contain examples of wood sculpture which are notable for delicacy and individuality of conception and masterly skill in the use of polychrome painting *(Plate p. 93)*.

The foreign sculptors who came to Russia in the early years of the century — Nicolas Pineau, Andreas Schlüter, Konrad Osner and others — made relatively little contribution to the development of Russian plastic art. The only one of them to achieve a position of any prominence in the history of Russian sculpture was Carlo Rastrelli (1675-1754), who found in Russia a second home and wide scope for the employment of his gifts. He was a prolific worker in the most varied genres, but it was in the field of portrait sculpture that he showed the full measure of his talent. An outstanding example of his work is his famous bust of Peter the Great, an entirely convincing presentation of the dynamic figure of the Emperor. Designed for effect but yet profoundly true to life, filled with the fierce energy and resolution of the sitter, this work represented an entirely new achievement in portrait sculpture. Other important works by Rastrelli which have survived are a bust of Prince A. Menshikov, a statue of the Empress Anna, a self-portrait and some decorative sculpture. Although not remarkable for psychological insight or delicacy of modelling, Rastrelli's works were valued for their undoubted professionalism, a quality which Russian sculpture was still striving to attain.

Rastrelli's name is linked with the history of two major monuments which were conceived in the early years of the century. The first of these is the so-called "Triumphal Pillar", a work dating from Peter's reign on which Rastrelli was engaged along with Andrey Nartov and Nicolas Pineau. This was to be a tall column entirely covered with reliefs representing incidents from the Northern War, the foundation of St Petersburg and other events. Unfortunately a variety of circumstances prevented the execution of this project, and the column exists only in the form of a model; but even this conveys a clear impression of the outstanding qualities of the design.

Rastrelli's other large monumental work, which he was able to bring almost to completion, was an equestrian statue of Peter the Great. A large model of the monument was completed before the

sculptor's death; but although the statue was cast in bronze it was not erected and was lost to sight for many years. Then, in the 1760s, when it was again proposed to erect a monument to Peter the Great, it was decided not to use Rastrelli's work. In the second half of the century Peter was thought of mainly as a wise statesman and legislator, the man who had transformed and modernised Russia; and accordingly Rastrelli's horseman was not thought appropriate to the occasion. Thereafter the statue was again forgotten until the very end of the century, when its existence was remembered almost by accident; and in 1800, on the directions of the Emperor Paul I, it was at last erected in front of the Engineers' Castle (formerly the Michael Castle).

The achievement of Russian art in the early 18th century were made possible by the cultural development of the previous century. The rich traditions inherited from the past continued to develop in the new conditions, preserving the essential homogeneity of Russian art and giving it a marked national individuality.

III   THE MID EIGHTEENTH CENTURY

The period after Peter the Great's death was a difficult one for Russia. A struggle for power began, one court faction ousted another, foreigners gained increased influence, and the headlong tempo of the early years of the century gave place to a more moderate pace. The substitution of one ruler for another, however, could not hold up the historical process. The country went through a particularly difficult time during the reign of the Empress Anna, when the prodigal luxury of court life was in glaring contrast with the poverty of the ordinary people and the Empress's foreign favourites rose to unprecedented influence, so that in effect it was they who governed the country. A reflection of this period can be seen in Carlo Rastrelli's sculptured group "The Empress Anna" *(Plate p. 128)* — in the sombre grandeur of the conception, the splendour of the Empress's elaborate dress, well expressing the character of the "Empress with the fearful glance", as she was called. A degree of stability was achieved only with the accession of Peter's daughter Elizabeth in 1741.

In the history of Russian art the post-Petrine period is sometimes considered an age of decline. This is a misconception. Art continued to develop, and nothing could halt its advance. No doubt there was a slackening of pace, but that was all. During this period a number of great decorative painters and portraitists were at work, and architecture continued to progress.

The middle of the 18th century was a period of great achievement in Russian architecture. There was much building of palaces and large churches, and the baroque style came to full flowering. Luxurious palaces, lavishly decorated with carving and painting, and splendid parks were created to meet the

needs of the Imperial court and the great feudal magnates; but in this period much less effort went into the erection of public buildings.

In the buildings of this period the decorative sculpture formed an important part of the total architectural effect and was conceived as an integral part of the whole. Architects made extensive use of architectural details — pilasters, half columns, columns and round pediments — to create an impression of splendour and magnificence. The decorative effect of mid 18th century architecture was still further enhanced by the use of colour to set off the purely plastic qualities of the structure.

In this period, too, were created the great parks at Kuskovo near Moscow, Tsarskoe Selo near St Petersburg, and elsewhere, which demonstrated the pre-eminent skill of Russian landscape gardeners.

An outstanding architect who left his distinctive mark on the architecture of the period was Bartolommeo Rastrelli (1700-71), son of the sculptor. In this earliest buildings he still showed restraint in the use of decorative elements, introducing pilasters and occasionally vertical ribs of rusticated stone but only rarely employing sculptured ornament. Already, however, he had developed the conception of a building designed for purposes of display, in which he was later to demonstrate his matchless skill. Typical examples of his work are the Vorontsov Palace (Leningrad) and the reconstruction of the Great Palace at Peterhof. In the interior of the palace at Peterhof, with its profusion of carved ornament, the wealth of applied decoration created the effect of magnificence and graceful elegance which is characteristic of Rastrelli's style. This building was already the work of a mature artist with a fully developed mastery of technique and a considered view of the function of architecture.

In the later 1740s Rastrelli's work showed the full measure of its achievement. To this period belong his best known buildings — the Winter Palace, the Catherine Palace at Pushkin (formerly Tsarskoe Selo) and the Smolny Convent in St Petersburg.

In the Catherine Palace *(Plates pp. 102, 105)* Rastrelli was faced with the task of incorporating various structures belonging to the old palace in a new building of tremendous size, in such a way as to achieve a homogeneous style and an impression of magnificence. Suites of reception rooms, conceived as a unified whole, lead to the Throne Room, and this sequence of rooms constitutes the principal feature of the palace. The elegant doors with their elaborate decorative mouldings, the ceilings with their riot of carved and gilded ornament, and the exquisite parquet flooring combine to create an effect of elegant splendour; and the exterior, with its colour wash of white and blue, its gilding and its Atlas figures, is no less impressive.

The Winter Palace *(Plate p. 108)* is another building of great magnificence. It consists of a square range of buildings surrounding a grand courtyard, with extensions at the four corners. The columns

on the external walls and the carved decoration of the cornices are very characteristic of Rastrelli's style and enhance the effect of richness and splendour. The interior was designed in the same baroque style, but a century later, in 1837, it suffered serious damage in a fire and was reconstructed. Standing as it does at the very centre of the city, the Winter Palace is an impressive demonstration of the high level of achievement attained by Russian architecture in the 18th century.

Finally we have another magnificent example of Rastrelli's skill in the Smolny Convent *(Plates pp. 110, 111)*. He was unable to finish the building, though we can judge the quality of his design from the model which has been preserved; but even in its present form Smolny is a building of remarkable originality and talent. The cathedral in particular achieves an admirable unity between the masses of the interior and the articulation of the exterior. The lavish ornament was designed to make the building stand out against its surroundings, and the bell-tower to give it the necessary magnificence. The whole building is remarkable for its lightness, its soaring upward movement, and its relationship with its environment — all achieved by a carefully considered distribution of volumes.

In addition to his work in St Petersburg Rastrelli did much building in other cities — in Moscow, Kiev and the Baltic area. An outstanding example of his work is the Cathedral of St Andrew in Kiev, which has become an integral part of the city pattern and contributes a distinctive feature to its skyline.

Other architects were also active at this period, producing a large number of notable buildings. Among them was Savva Chevakinsky (1713 to after 1783), who designed the Naval Cathedral of St Nicholas in St Petersburg *(Plates pp. 112, 113, 114)*. Basically cruciform in plan, this five-domed church stands in a large square and is one of the finest buildings in the city. It is notable for its large carved iconostasis, which lends a unique beauty to the interior.

Leading Moscow architects of this period were Ivan Michurin (1703-63), who made lavish use of decoration in his buildings, and his pupil Dmitry Ukhtomsky (1719-75). Ukhtomsky continued the construction of the famous bell-tower of the Monastery of the Trinity and St Sergius (Zagorsk), which was begun by Michurin *(Plate p. 115)*. Starting with a massive foundation structure, he erected on this a series of four stories of progressively diminishing size, pierced with arches and with columns at the angles: a design which gave the tower the elegance and the soaring upward movement characteristic of baroque architecture. With its beauty of proportion and graceful design the bell-tower is one of the finest achievements of mid 18th century Russian architecture. Ukhtomsky occupies an important place in the history of Russian architecture as a great tea-

cher, the founder of an architectural training school which produced many distinguished architects, including Vasily Bazhenov, Matvey Kazakov and Aleksandr Kokorinov.

Among other architects who were active in the middle of the century were Andrey Kvasov, who designed a large cathedral in Kozelets (Ukraine), and Fëdor Argunov, who built the Sheremetev Palace in St Petersburg and a country residence for the same family at Kuskovo on the outskirts of Moscow.

The complex of buildings and parks at Kuskovo is a typical example of the type of suburban establishment favoured by the nobility in this period *(Plates pp. 116-123)*. Kuskovo is a rare example of a successful synthesis between architecture and the countryside, between painting and sculpture, which has preserved all the atmosphere and flavour of the 18th century. The palace itself is typical of the architecture of the period, with its reception rooms arranged *en suite* and its lavish use of sculpture

111

and painting for decorative purposes. The whole place is a museum full of valuable works of art. The palace is not, however, an isolated element in the over-all design, but stands in an organic relationship with the park, the lake, the avenues of trees and the shrubbery. The decorative sculpture in the park, the vases and the ornamental railings give Kuskovo its particular charm and its special flavour of the past. Work on the palace and the park continued throughout the 18th century, but the bulk of the building was completed between the 1750s and the 1770s.

Another outstanding example of the same style is the palace of Ostankino on the outskirts of Moscow *(Plates pp. 124-127).*

The middle of the 18th century saw a particular flowering of decorative sculpture, which was widely used in many baroque palaces and public buildings which are remarkable for their magnificence of proportions and luxuriance of ornament. Perhaps at no other period in the history of Russian architecture was such lavish use made of plastic ornament in architecture. The work of Bartolommeo Rastrelli is a perpetual demonstration of the use of sculpture for the internal and external decoration of buildings. In the Catherine Palace at Pushkin sculptured detail sometimes takes the place of architectural detail as a means of creating a particular decorative and plastic emphasis at the most important points in the design. The massive Atlas figures on the ground floor form a strong three-dimensional element to which the whole plastic pattern of the façade seems to be related. Along with the more restrained design of the first floor and the mouldings of the cornices and pediments, this profusion of plastic ornament creates an effect of elegance and gaiety. With all its exuberance, however, the sculptured decoration of Russian baroque buildings never obscures the rhythm or functional quality of the structure. There is a similar profusion of sculpture in the interior of the building. Intricate mouldings provide a frame of exquisite elegance for the panels of painted decorations. Here again the sculpture, without losing its own independence, plays an important part in bringing out the full significance of the architectural conception.

The baroque style is mainly based on the exploitation of plastic form, with its dynamism, its cascade of three-dimensional masses and its dramatic interplay of light and shade. It is a world of restless movement in which only the functional requirements of the architecture restrain the unending flow of sculptural form and give it the necessary logical pattern.

A leading figure in the world of painting in the middle of the century was Ivan Vishnyakov (1699-1761), an accomplished decorative artist and portrait painter. As a decorative painter he took part in the decoration of many buildings in St Petersburg and the surrounding area; as a portraitist he is particularly known for his portraits of William and Sarah Fermor (Russian Museum).

His portrait of Sarah Fermor (c. 1750) *(Plate p. 134)* is one of his most delightful works. At first glance there seems to be nothing new about the composition of the picture: a column, a vista of landscape, a canopy, providing a background for the standing figure of a girl — elements which are common enough in portraits of this period. The representation of the figure, however, is a work of exquisite skill. Sarah Fermor, wearing the splendid dress of a lady of fashion, complete with wig and fan, is full of vivid reality and poetic truth. Her wide eyes gaze demurely out of the picture. The consciously elegant position of her arms and the rather constrained pose do not detract from the naturalness of the portrait. In spite of the formal setting the personality of this young girl, scarcely more than a child, emerges clearly from the picture. Vishnyakov has caught all the charm of youth and embodied it with great delicacy in his portrait.

It is characteristic of the period that the portrait still retains something of the style of the *parsuna* — a rigidity of pose, a certain flatness of form, a concern with the rendering of ornament. The flowers on Sarah Fermor's dress are scattered over the surface of the material with little regard for three-dimensional form, in the manner familiar to us from the *parsuna*. This mingling of old and new, however, merely enhances the charm of the work. The artist's skill is also shown in the use of colour, based on a subtle interplay of tones of pearly white. Vishnyakov was a painter of great individuality and technical mastery whose work has not yet been adequately studied; but there can be no doubt of his standing as an artist and as a representative of his period.

The work of Vishnyakov and his contemporaries shows that the traditions of the *parsuna* in portrait painting had not been completely displaced in the earlier part of the century. These traditions proved extraordinarily tenacious, continuing for many years to exist and to exert influence on artists. It is sometimes suggested that the pattern of Russian art was set by these traditional features, which maintained its link with icon-painting and the conventional style of the *parsuna*. This is, however, an erroneous view. In the early years of the century Russian painting had turned away from the conventionality of religious art and entered a new channel of development. Artists were now faced with fresh tasks, and the essential qualities of their work are to be seen not in the elements of artificiality which they inherited from the past but in their much more subtle revelation of character and in their entirely secular conception and realistic expression of human personality.

As another example of this we may consider one of Vishnyakov's contemporaries, Aleksey Antropov (1716-95), on whom the traditions of the *parsuna* also had their effect. He too was active as a decorative painter, and among other work was responsible for the decoration of the Cathedral of St Andrew in Kiev during the 1750s.

At one time Antropov was principal artist to the Holy Synod, in which capacity he supervised the work of the icon-painters and did a fair amount of icon-painting himself. Inevitably this had an effect on his portraits, in which the older ideas are still strongly reflected. As an example of his work we may take his portrait of "Ataman Krasnosh-chekov" (Russian Museum) (*Plate p. 135*), which shows the rigidity of pose and concern with orna-ment characteristic of the *parsu-na*. Krasnoshchekov's garments are adorned with a flowered

brocade pattern, painted flatly with no attempt at a three-dimensional effect, and his face, with its prominent eyes and curving moustaches, is rigid and almost expressionless.

There are also some portraits by Antropov in a freer style, less subject to the influence of the *parsuna*.

Another very gifted artist of this period was Ivan Argunov (1727-1802). He was a serf of the Sheremetev family, and his career is a reminder of the difficulties and hardships besetting any serfs who showed talent in one direction or another. There were composers, actors, architects and artists of considerable quality who, as serfs, had received training at their masters' expense, but were completely without civil rights and could be sold or exchanged at their owner's whim like ordinary goods or chattels. The consequences were frequently tragic, involving the destruction of a promising talent. The history of Russian art in this period is full of cases of this kind.

Ivan Argunov suffered all the difficulties and tribulations of a serf in this situation, compelled to humour his master's every whim. Many of his portraits had to be painted from a model, for the great magnates of the day thought it beneath their dignity to sit for a portrait painted by a serf, even when he was a gifted artist. When Argunov was at the height of his powers he was transferred by the Sheremetev family from St Petersburg to Moscow to be the majordomo of their palace there, and in consequence had to devote his energies to domestic business and almost abandoned painting.

Argunov's portraits show the same transitional features as those of his contemporaries. In his early works the older conceptions of form are still prominent, but as time went on his style gained in depth and showed increased delicacy and technical skill. Thus in his portrait of Princess Lobanov-Rostovsky the static and ornamental elements are predominant, but in the portraits of an unknown sculptor and his wife (Russian Museum) and even more strikingly in his "Peasant in Russian Costume" (Tretyakov

Gallery) Argunov shows affinities with the leading artists of the second half of the century. In these works he achieves much greater freedom and independence as an artist, in his striving to reach the fullest understanding of the character of his sitters. Argunov's development is very characteristic of the period as a whole: Russian portrait painting was making steady progress towards an understanding of human psychology and was now able to convey more accurately than ever before the essence of a sitter's character and disposition.

In 18th century Russia there was one flourishing branch of art which has now fallen into decline — the art of preparing and organising festivities and celebrations of all kinds. Prodigies of skill were lavished on triumphal buildings, arches, pavilions, masquerades, and above all on fireworks. There is plentiful evidence of all this in contemporary pictures and prints, and also in the memoirs and letters of the period. The leading poets, writers and artists of the day took part in the organisation of these festivities, devoting all the resources of their imagination and taste to the creation of a splendid ceremonial occasion.

One characteristic and important genre of Russian art is represented by the popular prints known as *lubki* (in the singular *lubok*), which appeared for the first time in the second half of the 17th century and rapidly became popular with the mass of the population. These cheap prints, containing an easily intelligible text, often of a satirical character and sometimes devoted to actual events of the day, found a ready sale and penetrated into the remotest corners of the country.

118

The *lubki* were printed from wood blocks and then coloured. Their crudeness of style was well adapted to the tastes of their audience, and the text was frequently phrased in the language of the Russian folk tales. They were not merely a source of comfort and education for the ordinary people of Russia but were themselves works of folk art, being produced by craftsmen who belonged to the people. It was in the 18th century that they achieved their greatest flowering.

An event of great significance in the history of Russian art in the 18th century was the foundation of the Academy of Arts in St Petersburg in 1757.

The need for a professional art school had been acutely felt as early as the beginning of the 18th century. Until then there had been no centralised arrangements for the training of artists, which had been left to a variety of local groups or "teams" of artists, as they were called. At the beginning of the century there had been a school attached to the St Petersburg printing-house, and at a later stage art classes were organised by the Academy of Science; but these were merely expedients which did not meet the real need. It was essential to have a proper art school, a single establishment responsible for providing training for students in the various arts and crafts.

The Russian Academy was established in 1757 and very rapidly developed into one of the leading art schools of the world. It achieved unquestioned authority, the results of its work received general recognition, and it was no accident that some of its students who were sent to France and Italy with State bursaries were elected to honorary membership of the leading European academies of art.

The organiser of the Russian Academy was Ivan Shuvalov, an enlightened statesman and one of the most cultured men of his day, and its inspiration came from the great Russian scholar Mikhaylo Lomonosov. The 18th century was of course much concerned with education, and took a great interest in the various experiments through which it was hoped to evolve a rational and effective educational system; and Russian thinkers also were much exercised about the possibility of developing a form of teaching which should make it possible to "educate a new race of men free from the vices of contemporary society". With this in mind a training school was attached to the Academy, to which boys were admitted at the age of five or six. They remained at the school for fifteen years, following a curriculum which included education in general subjects but was principally devoted to the teaching of art.

To begin with a number of foreigners — Le Lorrain, Lagrenée, Torelli — were enlisted as teachers. Unfortunately they devoted too much time to private commissions and not enough to their teaching duties, and within two years gave up their posts, leaving nothing to show for their passage. A greater contribution was made by the French sculptor Nicolas Gillet, whose studio turned out a group of distinguished sculptors. A decisive part in the establishment of art teaching in Russia was also played by Anton Losenko, a historical painter. After the early years teaching posts at the Academy were occupied by such outstanding artists as Shubin, Martos, Gordeev, Kozlovsky, Akimov, Ugryumov, Levitsky and Kokorinov, among many others.

Throughout the 18th century the authority of the Russian Academy stood high. It maintained close connections with various foreign academies and could count among its members many European artists and writers of the highest eminence such as Boucher, Falconet and Diderot. It was not merely the leading professional school but a vital centre of artistic life, since it included within its membership almost all the Russian artists of any importance, and thus exercised a very considerable influence on the artistic life of Russia.

IV   THE FLOWERING OF EIGHTEENTH CENTURY ART

The second half of the 18th century is a period of great interest in the history of Russian art, a period when many great painters, sculptors and architects were at the height of their powers, in which a whole new school of artists came to maturity.

It was also a period of important developments in both the internal and external affairs of Russia. In foreign affairs it saw the conclusion of the Seven Years' War, the partition of Poland and the recovery of Russian territory in western Belorussia, and the war with Turkey, then in an expansionist mood. The victories of Russian arms on both land and sea greatly enhanced the country's international prestige.

The internal history of Russia during this period was no less eventful. Throughout the century there were recurrent "troubles", and there was a persistent current of unrest over the evils of serfdom. Catherine II directed all her efforts to strengthening the feudal nobility, granting them far-reaching privileges, and

the serfs lost any claim to government protection. "In the eyes of the law the peasants were dead": Radishchev's phrase was entirely apt.

The inevitable consequence of this policy was the Peasant War, the rising led by Emelyan Pugachëv. The events of the war, which shook the Empire and were followed with eager interest by the whole of Russia, represented an important stage in the struggle against the enslavement of the peasants. The more liberal elements among the nobility were powerless to make any effective contribution to the solution of the peasant problem. References to the hardships of the peasants are found in the works of many writers and poets of this period: for example, we find Mikhail Chulkov, Vladimir Lukin, Fëdor Emin and — most significantly of all — Denis Fonvizin and Nikolay Novikov attacking the arbitrary behaviour of the landowners and describing the grievous slavery to which the peasants were reduced.

There was a striking contrast between the unbridled luxury of the feudal aristocracy and the destitution of the ordinary people. Something like 800,000 serfs were distributed by Catherine to members of the nobility; and the nobles were also granted numerous privileges which ensured their loyal support for the autocratic Imperial regime.

A further scourge which afflicted the country at this period was the swarm of royal favourites. Catherine had a whole series of such favourites, who enriched themselves at the country's expense,

124

receiving presents in the form of large estates and thousands of State-owned peasants. The Orlov brothers alone received more than 50,000 peasants from Catherine at various times.

Moreover the feudal nobility's pursuit of luxury was combined with a contempt for all things Russian, and their emulation of foreign fashions caused great harm to the development of the national culture.

The sixties and early seventies of the 18th century represented the first stage in the Russian "Enlightenment", when men like Yakov Kozelsky, Nikolay Novikov and Nikolay Kurganov were actively engaged in the movement.

In the 1770s the figurative arts took a great stride forward. New genres were established, the principles of realism triumphed in painting and sculpture, and the historical genre made important progress. The artist's concern to lay bare man's inmost nature, to comprehend his character and produce a true likeness in painting or sculpture was paralleled by the efforts being made by the thinkers of the Enlightenment to achieve recognition of the materialistic approach to knowledge and to establish a system of human values which transcended class. The association between the Enlightenment and the arts is so evident that even the gulf between literature and journalism on the one hand and painting and sculpture on the other creates no obstacle to an understanding of the essential unity of this process in the history of Russian culture.

Argunov, Rokotov, Levitsky, Shubin and Losenko — each in his own way according to the measure of his talent — penetrated into the inmost essence of human character, studied all its varied aspects, and produced portraits informed by a profound humanist understanding which achieve a powerful effect not only by their external resemblance but by their intensity of inner life. The central figure in 18th century Russian art, the embodiment of its social and aesthetic ideal, became the living, thinking human being.

Eighteenth century Russian art had close links with the art of the other peoples who formed part of the Russian Empire. The capital of the country, St Petersburg, attracted many gifted artists, who were trained in the Academy of Arts and then either returned to their home district to work or found employment in the capital. There were particularly strong and fruitful links between Russia and the Ukraine. Many Ukrainians received their professional training in Russia, and some of them subsequently made their contribution to Russian culture: we need only think, for example, of Dmitry Levitsky, Vladimir Borovikovsky and Ivan Martos. The community of interest between the various peoples was quite evident. It is important to note, however, that this was not a one-sided process in which Russian art influenced the art of the other peoples, but a constant two-way interchange. Ukrainian art, for example, had considerable influence on the art of Russia: thus the development of Russian portrait painting in the 18th century shows clear evidence of influence from the Ukrainian school of portrait painting. And this is true in varying degree of the art of the other peoples of Russia.

According to 18th century ideas the supreme artistic genre was the historical genre. The representation of the heroes of the past was accepted as the noblest task of the artist, for the exploits of these heroes overshadowed the deeds of contemporaries and were well calculated to inspire a sense of patriotism, respect for the achievements of the past, love of country, and noble and lofty sentiments. Every encouragement was therefore given to the development of historical painting and sculpture, and the work of practitioners in these genres was extravagantly praised. In comparison with this work the arts of portrait and landscape painting were regarded as being of secondary importance.

The origins of the historical genre — which at this time was widely defined to include mythological and religious as well as purely historical themes — are to be sought in the work of the Academy of Arts during the second half of the century.

The first, and the most important, figure in the field of historical painting was Anton Losenko (1737-73). Born in the Ukraine, he became a boy chorister in a court choir, and later was taken into

Argunov's studio. He remained only a
year in the Academy and then spent some
years in France and Italy. On his return
he painted two pictures — "Vladimir and
Rogneda", on a theme from Russian history,
and "Hector's Farewell to Andromache",
on a theme from the *Iliad*. Both pictures
now seem to us to contain many archaic
features, but in their day they made a
great impression as the first paintings in modern Russian art devoted to particular narrative themes. Losenko's works, and particularly his life studies, were admired for their
perfection of technique and were frequently
used as models by students in the Academy.

The distinctive feature of Losenko's
work is his concern with Russian subject
matter, and his special achievement is to
have established the status of the historical
genre as the highest expression of the painter's art. We have already noted his importance as a teacher; and he was also one of the
most accomplished draughtsmen of his day.

The main achievements of 18th century Russian art, however, were in the field of portraiture.
During this period Russian portrait painters enormously extended their technical range and their
ability to reveal all the complexities of human character. Compared with the figures depicted by the
historical painters, with their considerable element of abstraction and conventionality, portrait painting
was an art of great vitality, pulsating with life and infinitely varied. This was the genre which surpassed
all others in expressing the manifold facets of human personality. The process of establishing the value
of personality in opposition to the art of the Middle Ages, which had begun in the 17th century, reached
its logical culmination in the art of the portrait painters of the second half of the 18th.

Fëdor Rokotov was one of the outstanding painters of the second half of the century. Until recently
his name was surrounded by an aura, if not of mystery at least of ignorance. During the 19th century

he was almost forgotten. The private collections of many noble families no doubt contained paintings by this very individual artist — portraits, now dark with age, of men and women belonging to an era long past. The patina of time concealed the qualities of Rokotov's work from later generations: collectors took no interest in his paintings, and no one seems to have made any effort to discern the real gifts which they displayed.

Then all of a sudden, at the turn of the 19th and 20th centuries, Rokotov's work was rediscovered and aroused enthusiastic interest among art lovers. His pictures were displayed at exhibitions, and the public were able to appreciate their strikingly individual use of colour, their originality of manner and their technical accomplishment. In consequence they now began to be much sought after by collectors. At that time there were only three or four of his works in the Russian Museum, the remainder being in private hands.

Until quite recently nothing was known about the artist's origins, where he received his training, the dates of his birth and death, or the story of his life; but although there are still many gaps in our knowledge of Rokotov's career there is now general agreement on his stature as one of the outstanding figures of 18th century portrait painting — an artist of great originality who played an important part in the development of the genre.

Fëdor Rokotov (1735-1808) came of a serf family, and we still do not know who gave him his first training as a painter. In 1760 he was admitted to the Academy of Arts and soon became a teacher there; but even before entering the Academy he had acquired a considerable reputation and was in great demand in St Petersburg as a portrait painter. In 1765, after being granted the title of Academician, he left St Peters-

burg and returned to his native Moscow, where he painted most of the works to which he owes his fame.

Rokotov was a master of the "chamber portrait" — usually a head-and-shoulders representation in which the artist's attention was concentrated on the sitter's face. We also have a number of full-dress portraits by him, including a state portrait of the Empress Catherine, the first to be painted after her coronation in Moscow. But this genre did not appeal to Rokotov, and did not bring out his finest qualities. He was most at home with the chamber portrait, and it was in works of this kind that his understanding of human character and his aesthetic principles found their fullest expression.

Rokotov's portraits are of such striking individuality that they cannot be mistaken for the work of any other artist. His basic objective was to reveal the inmost personality of the sitter, and in particular his emotional mood. The figure, lit by a soft light, is almost always shown in a lively and colourful setting, and there is often a slight smile playing round the subject's mouth. The outer corners of the eyes are emphasised by delicate brush-strokes which tone down the highlights and give the sitter's glance a certain reticence and emotional force. While fully preserving the individuality of the sitter's features Rokotov is concerned to bring out his intelligence and sensibility. We can see this in his portraits of Vasily Maykov, the writer (1765, Tretyakov Gallery) *(Plate p. 132)*, A. Vorontsov (1760s, Tretyakov Gallery), N. Struysky (1772, Tretyakov Gallery), Surovtsev (1780s, Russian Museum) and many others.

Rokotov was particularly skilled in the painting of women. His female figures radiate a sense of virtue and purity, of dignity and humanity; and yet behind the simplicity and naturalness of their smile there is almost always an element of mystery, a hidden significance which gives the portrait the distinctive touch we recognise as characteristic of Rokotov's work. Among the best of his female portraits are those of Mme Struysky (1772, Tretyakov Gallery), Mme Surovtsev (1780s, Russian Museum), Mme Orlov (1779, Tretyakov Gallery), Mme Santi (1785, Russian Museum) *(Plate p. 136)* and Mme Novosiltsev (1780, Tretyakov Gallery).

Rokotov's portraits always show a very individual use of colour and rendering of material. The broadcloth and velvet of a man's waistcoat, the embroidery on his coat, the lace or gauze of his jabot, and the satin and silk of a woman's dress are painted with swift and delicate brush-strokes. In his handling of material Rokotov is not concerned to lay any particular stress on the outlines; but there is no loss of solidity, since the substance of the material is expressed by skilful use of pure painting techniques. In this respect Rokotov stands out from his contemporaries.

Rokotov thus achieved a new and important advance in the art of portrait painting, gaining an insight into the world of human personality and revealing the spiritual beauty and perfection to which it can attain.

A contemporary of Rokotov's who also gained a great reputation as a portrait painter was Dmitry Levitsky. His work is an important contribution to 18th century Russian realism and represents a considerable advance in the development of the genre. Although in the second half of the century, as in earlier years, a number of foreign portrait painters were at work in Russia — including in particular Louis Tocqué, Georg Groot, Pietro Rotari and Stefano Torelli — there were fewer of these incomers than in the first half of the century. In this period, therefore, the achievement of Russian artists takes on quite different dimensions. Their considerable technical accomplishment, their accumulated experience and their high professional standards enabled many of them to vie with the accepted foreign masters of the day. One Russian artist who not only bore comparison with foreign artists but surpassed many of them in skill was Levitsky, a magnificent draughtsman and painter who in the course of his long life painted a whole series of portraits which reflected the spirit of the age and recorded for posterity the likeness of many of his contemporaries.

Dmitry Levitsky (1735-1822) was born in the Ukraine, the son of an engraver, and received his first professional training from his father. Then in the 1750s, when the Cathedral of St Andrew in Kiev was being decorated by a group of artists under the direction of Antropov, the young Levitsky was included in the team. Subsequently he moved to St Petersburg, where he continued to be a pupil of Antropov's. He made his debut as a portrait painter at an exhibition in the Academy of Arts in 1770, when he showed a number of portraits, including one of Aleksandr Kokorinov, the architect who was also Director of the Academy *(Plate p. 137)*. The professional mastery shown in this work, its fine draughtsmanship, its accuracy in reproducing the likeness of the sitter and the skill with which it gave naturalness to an official portrait were immediately recognised and acclaimed. Levitsky thereupon

received official recognition, being elected an Academician and appointed professor of portrait painting. During the 1770s he reached the peak of his powers. It was at this period that he painted the small but very expressive portrait of Diderot *(Plate p. 139)*, who had come to St Petersburg on the invitation of Catherine II. Evidently Diderot himself thought highly of this picture, for he took it with him when he returned to France and it was the only portrait which he left to his sister in his will.

Levitsky is particularly known for his series of portraits of pupils at the Smolny Institute, a school for daughters of the nobility. He painted each of them in a different pose according to her particular interests: Mademoiselle Borshchov dancing, Mademoiselle Molchanov reading, Mademoiselle Alymov playing the harp. These portraits finally consolidated the artist's reputation, and henceforth he was recognised as the leading Russian portrait painter of the day.

In his portraits of members of the nobility or of friends or relatives Levitsky achieved not only an external likeness of the sitter but also an expression of his inmost being. He sought always to depict as exactly as possible the sitter's character and social position as well as his physical appearance. Thus in his portrait of the Empress's favourite, Lansky (1782, Russian Museum), Levitsky creates the image of a spoiled and empty-headed young man: behind the external magnificence depicted in this official portrait he lays bare the futility and fatuity of the sitter. But where Levitsky is dealing with a person of more substance, or one with whom he feels greater affinity, he seeks to bring out as fully as possible the warmth and humanity of the sitter. We can see this, for example, in his portraits of his daughter Agafya and his father, and in portraits of N.A. Lvov (1789, Tretyakov Gallery), N.I. Novikov (1797, Tretyakov Gallery) and M.I. Dmitriev (Tretyakov Gallery).

Levitsky's female portraits are full of charm. He painted many portraits of women, and in all of them, with his accustomed mastery, he succeeds in revealing fresh aspects of their character, new facets of their psychology. One of his most delightful works is his portrait of Mme Dyakov (1778, Tretyakov Gallery). Levitsky's acute observation of character is also seen in his portraits of Mme Naryshkin (1774, Louvre), Mme Arsentyev (1782, Louvre), Mme Bakunin (1782, Tretyakov Gallery), Mme Golitsyn (1781, Russian Museum), and many others.

The famous state portrait of Catherine II as a lawgiver, painted in the early 1780s (Tretyakov Gallery), enjoyed great popularity in its day. The majestic figure of the Empress, wearing a white satin dress, is shown against the background of a crimson canopy, standing at an altar, behind which is a marble statue representing an allegorical figure of Justice. The portrait is painted with consummate artistry, with a broad free brush, giving it a monumental unity and impressiveness appropriate to the subject. Levitsky's conception, which was enthusiastically acclaimed by contemporaries, idealised the Empress but at the same time depicted her as a representative of enlightened monarchy, the rôle in which she strove to appear in the eyes of the world.

141

Levitsky was one of the group of artists who in the second half of the 18th century definitively established Russian art, and portrait painting in particular, as a profoundly realistic art and set a high standard of professional competence. His work can stand beside the great masterpieces of European portrait painting: Russian portraiture, which had taken its first timid steps in the early years of the century, had now attained full maturity.

The third of the great Russian portrait painters of the second half of the century was Vladimir Borovikovsky (1757-1825). Like Levitsky, he was born in the Ukraine. In his youth he was an officer in the army, but later resigned his commission and devoted himself entirely to painting. He received his first training from his father, who was a painter, and began his career by painting icons, mural paintings in churches, and portraits. It is thought that he may have spent some time as a pupil of Levitsky's. At the end of the 1780s he arrived in St Petersburg, and the most fruitful period of his career began. His characteristic manner, the originality of his composition and his delicate sense of colour soon gained him a considerable reputation.

In the 1790s Borovikovsky created a very individual type of female portrait. The essential feature of this was the placing of the figure, usually a head-and-shoulders portrait, against a landscape background. These portraits of the 1790s, lyrical in mood and full of strong poetic feeling, are the painter's finest works.

As an example of this style we may take the portrait of Mademoiselle Lopukhin (1797, Tretyakov Gallery) *(Plate p. 141)*. The figure of the sitter, posed in front of a sunlit landscape, is full of the charm of youth and radiant with warm feeling. The slight smile playing round her lips and the demure glance suggest the tenderness and grace of her very feminine personality. In this work the artist shows great subtlety in expressing the lyrical mood of his model; and the effect is enhanced by the way in which he stresses the link between the young girl and the serene sunny landscape. This was a device of which Borovikovsky was very fond and which can be seen in many of his portraits.

The use of colour in this portrait is very characteristic of Borovikovsky's style. The combination of white, blue and pink in heightened tonality is a regular feature of his work, often achieving a powerful resonance. Sometimes his use of colour is reminiscent of the ceramic-painter or the miniaturist. It can also be a very effective means of suggesting the personality of his female sitters and bringing out their lyrical mood, their femininity and their charm.

The portrait of Mademoiselle Lopukhin is one of Borovikovsky's finest works, but there are many others of similar quality. The same subtlety in the rendering of the sitter's mood is seen in his portrait of Mademoiselle Arsenyev (1790s, Russian Museum) *(Plate p. 145)*, a saucy young lady in a straw hat holding the traditional apple in her hand. There are many similar portraits, for the artist's style and composition were evidently popular with his public. Within this pattern, however, Borovikovsky nevertheless contrived to suggest the varying characters and moods of his sitters—as we can see, for example, from his portraits of Mme Skobeev, Mademoiselle Dolgoruky and a peasant girl called Khristina from the town of Torzhok.

In the 1790s Russian literature came under the influence of the sentimental school which is particularly associated with the name of Karamzin. The arts were not affected by the movement to any great extent, and few traces of its influence can be found in the work of the artists of this period. To a limited degree, however, the art of portrait painting did show some reflection of this style. The influence of the sentimental school can perhaps be traced most clearly in certain of Borovikovsky's portraits in which the elegiac and poetic mood is particularly stressed—for example in his portraits of the Gagarin sisters and the Kurakin sisters.

Borovikovsky's male portraits strike an austerer note. They are less concerned to achieve a poetic effect, they show a more positive effort to reveal the inmost character of the sitter, and they have more variety of compositional pattern. Examples are the striking portrait of the Persian Prince Murtaza-Kuli-Khan, a heavily bearded figure in Oriental costume (Russian Museum), the merciless representation of the complacent Prince A. Kurakin, the "diamond prince", and the dashing figure of General Borovsyk, painted against the background of a battle scene.

In addition to his portraits Borovikovsky also did much religious painting. In particular he took part in the decoration of the Cathedral of Our Lady of Kazan in St Petersburg. This work did not, however, compare in importance with his portrait painting. He was one of the three great artists of the second half of the 18th century who enhanced the significance of the realistic portrait, emancipated it from the archaic features inherited from the past, and established the importance of the genre. During the 18th century Russian portrait painting had come a long way: starting from the rigid conventions of the *parsuna*, it had progressed towards a profound understanding of human nature and had shown itself able to depict all the complexities of human personality—the most difficult task with which an artist can be faced.

Rokotov, Levitsky and Borovikovsky were by no means the only painters of quality in the second half of the 18th century, but their great gifts and their technical virtuosity made them outstanding among their contemporaries. Their work had a great influence on the subsequent development of portrait painting in the 19th century.

Another genre which developed in the second half of the century was the art of landscape painting. This genre had indeed existed at an earlier stage in the development of Russian art — in the decorative painting and engraving of the first half of the century, for example — but in this earlier period it had been of secondary importance, sometimes no more than a form of applied art. Now, however, a group of landscape artists trained in the Academy of Arts raised the status of the genre to new heights. This development of landscape painting was connected with the new romantic attitude to nature which was characteristic of the period. At first, it is true, the genre was marked by a certain artificiality; but in the work of its leading practitioners it attained a high degree of expressiveness and truth to nature.

The founder of the new genre was Semën Shchedrin (1745-1804), who had received his training in the Academy. In his pictures he depicted the parks and palaces of Pavlovsk, Gatchina, Peterhof and St Petersburg itself. His landscapes were usually built up on the basis of linear perspective, with the view framed between lateral features in the foreground. The use of colour was fairly conventional, with warm tones of brown predominating in the foreground, different shades of green in the middle distance, and cold blue tones in the background. This conventionality of colouring is found in most of the painters of the period, though there are certain exceptions to the rule. One of these who must be referred to is Fëdor Alekseev (1753-1824), a highly gifted artist who produced some fine views of St Petersburg. His pictures show a livelier use of colour, and his landscapes are inhabited by real people, the ordinary citizens of the town going about their everyday business, which gives his paintings a great feeling of naturalness. Moreover, like other landscapists, he had a good eye for the shapes of buildings and for architectural detail, and faithfully recorded the new construction then taking place in St Petersburg.

But the new landscape painters did more than produce accurate pictures of many attractive corners of the Russian countryside: they also demonstrated the vitality and significance of the art of landscape painting, established its status as an independent genre, and prepared the way for its further development in the 19th century.

Even in the art of mediaeval Russia we find some elements of genre painting in icons and mural paintings. In depicting scenes from ordinary life these earlier artists showed their interest in reflecting everyday reality and their dissatisfaction with an exclusively religious subject matter, seeking to give life to the imaginary events they depicted by showing the characters of the scriptural stories in real surroundings which would be familiar and comprehensible to the spectator.

The 18th century saw the emergence of genre painting as it is generally understood. In the middle of the century Ivan Firsov painted his picture of "The Young Painter", showing a young artist at his easel painting the portrait of a girl, perhaps his sister. The representation of the figures and the accurate rendering of the room and the still life on the table suggest that the picture was painted from life, and show an acute sense of observation. "The Young Painter" is a genre picture in the full meaning of the term.

Artists now began to show a lively interest in peasant life and manners. Foreign artists had long been aware of the rich store of subject matter to be found in Russia — the idiosyncrasies of Russian

144

character, the manners and customs of the people, the landscape. This is exemplified by the work of the French painter Jean Le Prince, who spent some years in Russia and painted a series of pictures of peasant life. Le Prince's work, however, was exceedingly remote from reality. What interested him was the exotic aspect of Russian life and manners, and in consequence his work lost all naturalness and truth to life. The peasant costumes became merely stage properties, the peasants themselves were mere lay figures, and scenes of everyday life were transformed into rather stilted pastorals. The result was quite without artistic value, as contemporaries noted: "The whole thing is cold, colourless, without expression," Diderot wrote about Le Prince's work.

Russian artists were, of course, better acquainted with the circumstances of peasant life under serfdom. A complete absence of civil rights, destitution, absolute dependence on the landowners — these were the realities of peasant life. To give artistic expression to these things was beyond the powers of the newly-fledged Russian realist school: this was a task reserved for the 19th century. But in the first half of the 18th century many painters took their subject matter from peasant life. One painter who dealt directly with this theme was Mikhail Shibanov, himself a serf belonging to the statesman G. A. Potëmkin. In one of his paintings, "The Peasants' Dinner", he showed a peasant family gathered round a table at their meagre meal. In this work, it is true, there is still no profound revelation of character; but at least the attempt had been made.

In another picture, "The Betrothal", Shibanov shows a party of peasants engaged in celebrating this traditional ceremony, a variegated group drawn together by the solemnity of the occasion and by the bond of tradition. The scene is depicted without embellishment; and we know from an inscription by the painter on the picture that it was painted from life.

The theme of peasant life was handled in an individual way by one of the most original and gifted artists of the 18th century, Ivan Ermenëv (1746 to after 1792). He had an unusual career, which is known to us only in the broadest outline. The son of a stableman who became a student at the Academy of Arts and was sent to Paris with a bursary from the Academy, Ermenëv was a witness of the French Revolution and recorded the fall of the Bastille in one of a series of drawings which were later engraved. Some of his allegorical pictures acquired a certain reputation, but it is not these that make him an important figure in the history of Russian art.

Returning to Russia, Ermenëv painted a series of water colours of peasant types. In these works there is no trace of the pastoral manner: they show the poor destitute wretches who were commonly to be met with on the roads of Russia in those days. One picture depicts a peasant dinner, and is in complete contrast to Shibanov's work. It shows the bare and comfortless log walls of a peasant *izba* and a crudely made table with a peasant family sitting silently round it eating hungrily out of a single dish, an expression of infinite weariness and foreboding on their faces. Another picture shows a group of blind beggars singing in a market-place — sitting in a circle dolefully intoning a melancholy song in the hope of attracting alms.

In a similar style are a series of drawings showing beggars and blind men travelling the roads with their knapsacks. These usually show one or two figures clad in filthy rags and tatters and carrying staffs in their hands, sometimes under the conduct of a leader, or single figures tramping from village to village in search of charity. They are depicted against a low horizon, which gives the figures increased significance and brings out more forcibly the tragedy of their situation.

All these pictures share the same artistic intention, and Ermenëv clearly demonstrates his sympathy with these outcasts in the hardships they have to endure. The drawings were done in the 1770s, at a time when many who had taken part in Pugachëv's unsuccessful peasant rising were still roaming aimlessly about the countryside. Not all of the drawings were finished, but all of them are clearly and carefully drawn — and all of them are a cry from the artist's heart.

We know little of Ermenëv's later career, but it seems to have ended tragically. After a further stay in France he returned to Russia, and appears to have died destitute and forgotten.

Russian genre painting was thus a creation of the 18th century. Slowly at first, but steadily, artists developed an interest in the life of ordinary people, and their work increased in quality and profundity. They thus prepared the way for the important development of genre painting in the early 19th century in the work of Aleksey Venetsianov and his school.

The second half of the 18th century also saw the formation of the Russian classical school. In the circumstances of Russian life it was natural that men should feel an urgent desire to set up a lofty ideal, a standard of perfection which was free from the sordidness of ordinary life and recalled the virtues of the great men of antiquity. The task of art was now to provide an education in citizenship and to promote patriotism, a sense of moral and public duty, and other civic virtues. The quest for perfect artistic models which should achieve these objectives led quite naturally to a remote period of antiquity, and to an art centred on the ideal of the free and harmoniously developed human being.

The classical style achieved its fullest expression in France, where its birth can be dated to the end of the 1760s and the early 1770s. During these years the last surviving remnants of the Rococo, the *rocaille* style, came under heavy attack, and the principles of the new school were established.

To the 18th century classicists ancient Greece and Rome were no mere fabulous world, and classicism itself was by no means an attempt to seek refuge in antiquity from the perplexing problems of contemporary life. Antiquity was thought of as an entirely concrete historical reality. No one doubted that the heroes of the Greeks and Romans had actually existed; no one questioned the existence of the free society in which they had lived and which had nurtured their heroic virtues. The remote past was seen as a fortunate period in human history, but a very real period which had been reflected in an out-pouring of perfect works of art. The world of the Bible was full of abstraction and unreality, but the world of antiquity was a real period in human history which had a meaning for the men of the modern world.

The culmination of the classical school in France was reached in the work of Louis David, with its profound social implications. His "Oath of the Horatii", "Death of Marat" and other remarkable works give expression to the progressive philosophy which was at the basis of the classical style.

Classicism developed in Russia at almost the same time as in France. In spite of the artificiality of dividing the history of art into periods, and the perennial controversies to which any attempt to do so gives rise, the origins of this style in Russia can reasonably be dated to the end of the sixties and the early seventies of the 18th century. The change can be clearly detected in architecture, sculpture and painting, in works by Vallin de la Mothe, Kokorinov, Gordeev, Losenko, Martos and Kozlovsky, among others, which show that the characteristics of the new school had not only attained a certain stability but had been welded into a recognisable unity of style.

Classicism in Russia was a style of great vigour and creative force which made a deep and lasting impression on Russian art. In the second half of the 18th century its influence was felt in every branch of art. Painting and sculpture, architecture and applied art, engraving and drawing — each of these genres, in varying degree, was caught up in the trend, and few indeed were the artists of the period who escaped the influence of the new style.

Russian classicism, however, was not in any sense a borrowing from the West. It was no mere import from Paris or Rome, brought back by travellers as the *dernier cri* of foreign fashion. It emerged in Russia as a necessary stage in the development of the national culture, as a logical consequence of the lofty objectives towards which progressive social and aesthetic thought in Russia was directed.

The influence of classicism was particularly marked in architecture, which succeeded in embodying the traditions inherited from antiquity in a characteristically national style of building. The process of development of the new style can be seen most clearly, therefore, in the field of architecture, where classicism launched a vigorous offensive against the Baroque, and the new principles rapidly found expression in the buildings of what is known as the "transitional period".

The days of remote antiquity were conceived as a time of freedom and independence for man, a time in which he was able to achieve the harmonious development of his personality and was free from the shackles of oppression. The real situation of the various social groups in the ancient world — the slavery, the predatory wars — was totally ignored. Russian artists were well acquainted with the history of ancient Rome and Greece: they had been familiar with it since their childhood, and they knew all about the heroes of antiquity and their exploits. Their vision of ancient history, however, took account only of its most striking aspects, seeing it as a period which attained a supreme develop-

ѲЕДОТЪ ШУБИНЪ
1792 ГОДА

ment of human personality, which created magnificent works of architecture and plastic art, which set a standard of high artistic achievement.

Russian classicism gave expression to the quest for social harmony, the lack of which was so clearly evident in Russia. The heroes of antiquity, those dwellers in a remote golden age, were seen as the antithesis to the bitter injustices and hardships of contemporary Russia. Just as in revolutionary France the classical style was adopted by the opponents of absolutism, providing them with the heroic attitudes and slogans in which they expressed their revolutionary fervour, so in 18th century Russia it became the vehicle for the lofty ideal which the progressive elements in Russian society were striving to realise.

The principal theme of Russian classicism was man, in whom the 18th century had boundless confidence. This belief in human destiny was indeed the supreme achievement of the century.

Winckelmann's definition of the qualities of classical art, "noble simplicity and tranquil grandeur", was not unquestioningly accepted by Russian artists. The vitalising link of art with everyday reality and the material world fostered the strain of realism which permeated Russian classicism and created its special national individuality. Losenko's "Hector", Gordeev's "Prometheus", Shchedrin's "Endymion", Ugryumov's "Yan Usmar", Kozlovsky's "Yakov Dolgoruky" and "Mounted Hercules" and many other works of the second half of the 18th century had a direct relevance to life, in both ideological content and artistic form. The distinctive feature of Russian classicism was that its practitioners were concerned not only with antiquity but with the history of their native land; and it was this that gave the works of the classical school their particular strength.

It must be remembered that in the second half of the 18th century classicism was by no means the only trend in Russian art. This was also the period of Shubin, Rokotov and Levitsky, whose work shows hardly a trace of classical influences and who nevertheless were among the leading artists of the day. The art of this period accommodated both a thoroughgoing realist like Shubin and a classicist like Kozlovsky; both of these artists gave full and personal expression to the aesthetic principles of the period, and both of them — notwithstanding their differences in artistic approach and in style — were profoundly involved in the life of that period.

An important part in the development of Russian sculpture was played by the Academy of Arts, which within ten years of its establishment had produced artists of the calibre of Fedot Shubin, Fëdor Gordeev, Mikhail Kozlovsky, Ivan Martos and Feodosy Shchedrin, among many others. The Academy actively promoted the development of the different sculptural genres, giving particular attention to carving in relief, which became very popular in the 18th century.

The outstanding achievement of Russian plastic art in the second half of the century lay in the field of portrait sculpture. The enhanced status which Rokotov, Levitsky and Borovikovsky had given the painted portrait was matched by a corresponding development of the sculptured portrait. It is significant that the portrait sculpture of this period was barely touched by the influence of classicism. The development of the portrait remained firmly within the traditions of realism; and however fervently an artist believed in the principles of classicism, immediately he turned to portraiture and was faced with the problem of representing the personality of a living human being in all its complexity he inevitably adopted a realistic approach.

Almost all the leading Russian sculptors of the period — Gordeev, Kozlovsky, Prokofyev, Martos and Shchedrin — were active in the field of portraiture, understood the specific requirements of the genre, and produced works of first-rate importance. The greatest contribution to the art of portrait sculpture, however, was made by Fedot Shubin (1740-1805), one of the outstanding figures in the history of Russian art.

Like Lomonosov, Shubin came from the White Sea area, and while still a boy became passionately interested in the art of carving, which was highly developed in this northern part of Russia; and after receiving his training at the Academy of Arts he retained a close link with folk art. An acute understanding of character, a remarkable psychological insight, an approach which varied according to the requirements of the particular portrait, and consummate technical skill: these are the qualities we find in Shubin's portraits. According to the aesthetic principles of the day the portrait was a genre of secondary importance; and it was Shubin, more than any of his contemporaries, who set the highest professional standards for this genre and established its aesthetic significance.

In his portrait sculpture Shubin shows a profound knowledge of life and of human character; he displays great variety and delicacy of perception, and can on occasion be quite merciless in his revelation of character. A striking example of his mature style is his portrait of Prince A. Golitsyn (1775, Tretyakov Gallery), a complex and fully rounded representation of a typical 18th century Russian magnate. Although compelled by circumstances to devote his talent to producing portraits of the feudal nobility, Shubin invariably achieves an acute and accurate insight into the character of his sitters and faithfully renders their personality and their inmost nature. This can be seen, for example, in such works as his portraits of members of the Orlov family, P. Sheremetev, G. Potëmkin, A. Bezborodko and E. Chulkov. Many of his portraits are imbued with a surprising warmth of feeling and a profound respect for his model — as, for example, in his portrait of Lomonosov (1790s, Academy of Science, Moscow) *(Plate p. 150)*, with whom he had much in common both in his career and in his attitude to life.

Shubin was one of those artists whose skill shows no sign of decline with advancing age, and only a year or two before his death he painted his famous portrait of Paul I (1801, Russian Museum), a masterpiece of Russian portrait sculpture *(Plate p. 151)*.

Shubin's portraits reflect all the variety of Russian character in his period, covering a wide range of age, temperament, experience and social position. He was a shrewd observer with a profound understanding of human nature; and his clear-sighted artistic vision enabled him to penetrate into the inmost recesses of a man's character, laying bare the essence of his being, concealed though it might sometimes be by outward appearances.

Shubin's work occupies a prominent place in any account of 18th century Russian art because his profound psychological insight enabled him to give expression to the aesthetic ideals which were central to the art of the period. In this respect Shubin's portraits are comparable with the best work of Rokotov, Levitsky and Borovikovsky.

One of the major events in the history of Russian sculpture was the erection of Etienne Maurice Falconet's famous statue of Peter the Great, representing him in the character of a great statesman and lawgiver; and the story of its creation is significant and instructive.

Throughout the 18th century the figure of Peter the Great had attracted the interest of many artists and his image had been reproduced in numerous portraits, busts, mosaics and engravings. It had also inspired two pieces of monumental sculpture. The first of these, by Carlo Rastrelli, has already been referred to. In the 1760s it appeared rather old-fashioned: the massive figure of the Tsar in his pompous attire was reminiscent of a Roman emperor, and this severe and majestic presence was quite out of line with the contemporary assessment of Peter's character and his contribution to the development of Russia. Peter was now recognised as a great statesman and lawgiver who had transformed the whole life of Russia; and this was how the public wanted to see their hero represented. Accordingly, on the recommendation of Diderot, a new statue was commissioned from Etienne Maurice Falconet (1716-91), an accomplished sculptor though admittedly with no experience of monumental sculpture, being known chiefly for his decorative sculpture, a statue of "Milon of Croton", and his designs for the Sèvres Manufactory. In spite of this limited experience, however, Diderot was able to perceive Falconet's undeveloped creative possibilities, his high professional gifts and his acute intelligence.

Falconet had made a profound study of the Petrine period. It happened that Voltaire, the "uncrowned king of Europe", had just published his *History of Russia in the Reign of Peter the Great*, which glorified Peter as a wise statesman, the "giant of the North". This was the first serious study of Peter published in a foreign country, a work based on authentic documents and free from the anecdotes and inventions which were so commonly found in books about Peter. Falconet knew Voltaire's work and undoubtedly learned a great deal from it. In addition, as he himself tells us, the ideas of the Russian "Enlightenment" played a great part in developing his conception of Peter. In expressing this conception in his statue he strove for the utmost simplicity and economy. "I am producing a statue of this hero," he wrote to Diderot, "representing him neither as a great commander nor as a conqueror — though of course he was both of these. Much more sublime is the character of the creator, the lawgiver, the benefactor of his country; and this is the character in which he must be represented."

This was the beginning of years of unremitting effort. Falconet produced a number of variations on the theme; a huge granite boulder weighing 100,000 poods was found, with considerable trouble, to serve as a pedestal; and unusual difficulties had to be overcome in the casting of the statue. Throughout the whole course of the work, indeed, innumerable difficulties were encountered; and although Falconet the artist was able to surmount them, Falconet the man, for all his resolution and directness of character, was powerless against the envy of his rivals and the hostility of courtiers. He was assisted in his work by Russian artists and bronze-founders and enjoyed the affection and respect of his fellow craftsmen, with whom he discussed every detail of the work as it progressed. Altogether the production of the statue took more than twelve years; but when the ceremonial inauguration took place in 1782 Falconet was not present, having already returned to France.

This statue of Peter the Great — the "Bronze Horseman", as it has been called since Pushkin wrote his famous poem with this title — became the emblem of St Petersburg *(Plate p. 155)*. The horse rearing up on its hind legs and the commanding figure of the Emperor were seen as a symbol of the new Russia, expressed with masterly skill in a composition of striking originality.

The effect of the statue is finely conveyed in Pushkin's lines:

> *Darkly it looms in terrifying power:*
> *What force of mind that brow conveys!*
> *What mighty strength lies there concealed!*
> *And in that horse what fire!*
> *Whither away, thou haughty steed?*
> *Where shall these proud hooves bear thee now?*

And thou, lord over destiny,
Didst thou not, with iron rein,
Pull Russia, rearing high,
Back from the brink of the abyss?

The statue conveys a powerful sense of dynamism, expressed in its soaring urgency of line and its unity of creative impulse. The horseman and the rock on which he stands are combined into a single significant whole; the bond between the statue and the pedestal here achieves a classical harmony. The simplicity and economy of the composition are matched by the simplicity and significance of the detail. The commanding gesture of Peter's right arm, full of powerful kinetic force, conveys all the nervous energy of the man. The whole conception of the statue is informed by the progressive ideology of the Enlightenment, presenting the monarch as a wise statesman, the "first citizen" of his kingdom, the guardian of legality and the educator of his people.

Falconet had no followers in Russia; but his immortal work provided an inspiring example of supreme craftsmanship which could not but be of benefit to the rising generation of Russian artists.

The Russian sculptors of the classical school produced works of great expressive power and high artistic quality. The leading representatives of this school were Fёdor Gordeev, Ivan Prokofyev, Ivan Martos, Feodosy Shchedrin and Mikhail Kozlovsky. Some of their sculpture still shows signs of baroque influence, but in their best works they express the aesthetic ideals of classicism.

The senior member of the group was Fёdor Gordeev (1745-1810), who was known for his "Prometheus" and a number of funerary monuments. He also produced a series of copies of works of ancient sculpture in which the originals were treated with considerable freedom.

Martos's funerary monuments, Shchedrin's "Venus" and "Diana", and a number of works by Prokofyev are instinct with the spirit of classicism, reflecting a varied and significant subject matter and expressing the ideology of humanism and the artists' striving to achieve supreme plastic perfection.

The leading sculptor of the closing years of the century was Mikhail Kozlovsky (1753-1802). An artist of great creative vigour and consummate professional skill, he produced a number of works which are entitled to a prominent place in the history of Russian sculpture. Perhaps more than any

other sculptor of the period he gave expression to the ideals of patriotism and the aspirations of his contemporaries. His "Mounted Hercules", "Yakov Dolgoruky", "Alexander the Great's Vigil" and other works show the powerful significance which Russian sculpture could now achieve.

Two works of outstanding importance produced by Kozlovsky shortly before his death are the statue of "Samson" in the famous Great Cascade at Peterhof and the monument to General Suvorov in Leningrad.

By the beginning of the 19th century the buildings, parks and fountains at Peterhof which had been created by Russian artists and craftsmen of the previous century had fallen into a state of neglect and dilapidation and were in need of restoration. The old lead statues which lined the cascades had also suffered from the effects of time and were on the point of complete collapse. It was decided, therefore, to replace all the statues which were beyond repair. This reconstruction of the cascade and the replacement of the old statues by new ones was an event of great importance in the history of Russian sculpture, and all the leading sculptors of the day, including Martos, Shubin, Shchedrin, Kozlovsky and Prokofyev, were enlisted in the task.

The operation was an extensive one, covering not only the casting of new statues from the old moulds but also the production of a number of new figures which transformed the whole decorative pattern of Peterhof. Prokofyev's "Perseus", "Sirens", "River Neva", and "River Volkhov", Shubin's "Pandora" and Martos's "Actaeon" enhanced the magnificence of the total effect, and the centrepiece of the whole design was provided by Kozlovsky's splendid statue of "Samson".

The figure of Samson is vibrant with inner force and commanding strength. The complex structure of this muscular body expresses infinite self-confidence, the resolution of the warrior and the triumph of the victor. His contest with the lion is interpreted by Kozlovsky in the spirit of the legendary hand-to-hand struggles which were a favourite theme of the old Russian epic tales; and this link with the traditional folk hero is reinforced by the fact that Samson is represented with the features of an ordinary Russian man of the people. Standing on an artificial rock in the centre of a basin, surrounded by the spray of the fountain, the bronze figure of Samson acquires added decorative and expressive force.

The culmination of Kozlovsky's achievement as a monumental sculptor is his statue of the great Russian commander General Suvorov *(Plate p. 152)*. Suvorov is represented in the pose of a real folk hero, holding his sword and shield, a figure of impetuous energy. The statue shows Kozlovsky's art at the stage of full maturity and at the peak of its artistic attainment. One of the most popular works of Russian monumental art, it demonstrates the high standard of accomplishment reached by Russian sculpture and represents in effect the final culmination of the process of development which it had passed through in the course of the previous century.

The 1760s and 1770s saw considerable changes in Russian architecture. The earlier concentration on palace building was no longer in accordance with the needs of the time. The towns were continuing to increase in size, and industry and trade were developing; and this made it necessary for architecture to turn in new directions. Public buildings, industrial installations and the problems of urban layout now received particular attention, and the building of splendid and pretentious palaces was no longer the architect's principal function. The development of architecture was increasingly influenced by the ideas of the Enlightenment and by the growing social and national awareness of Russian society. The quest for a new architectural ideal led in the direction of classicism and of the forms inherited from antiquity, with its rationalism and its austere and majestic ideal of beauty.

Although the building of palaces and churches still continued, the main emphasis now shifted to urban development. A special commission was established to prepare plans

for the development of the towns of Russia. The older parts of the towns were rebuilt and new quarters constructed; streets were straightened; the old fortifications were demolished; and a network of new main streets and squares was laid out. This happened not only in St Petersburg and Moscow but in many provincial towns. In this period, too, a new type of mansion — a large establishment standing in its own park — came into favour among the wealthy. The layout of the parks also changed, the old regular plan being replaced by the landscaped "English park". Formal geometric patterns gave place to the natural beauty of the countryside — even though this too might be created by the genius of the landscape gardener.

Architectural form now became increasingly dominated by the classical order, which gradually superseded the decorative features of the baroque style — though at first these continued in use.

One of the outstanding figures of these early days of classicism was the gifted architect Aleksandr Kokorinov (1726-72), who received his training in Ukhtomsky's school in Moscow and later moved to St Petersburg, where he established a thriving architectural practice. Kokorinov's finest building was the Academy of Arts, of which he was Director and the principal moving spirit during its early years. Lying on the banks of the Neva, it is notable for the originality of its internal layout, a clear-cut plan in which a large circular courtyard is enclosed within a rectangle. The main reception rooms lie along the principal front facing on to the Neva, with the studios and classrooms in the central part of the building. Kokorinov successfully solved the many problems of design arising from the use of the building for teaching — the studios, the classrooms, the exhibition halls, and so on. The serene rhythm of the façades expresses the internal structure; and the small projecting pavilions, decorated with columns, emphasise the severity of the main structure and create an impression of classical magnificence.

Another leading architect of this period was Vallin de la Mothe (1729-1800), who was invited to come to St Petersburg to teach in the Academy of Arts. He also had a part in designing the exterior of the Academy, but his talent came to full expression in the "Little Hermitage" which, in spite of its severity of line, achieved complete harmony with Rastrelli's adjoining Winter Palace. Another important building for which he was responsible was "New Holland", originally designed as a timber warehouse but never completed. The gateway, a masterpiece of disciplined form, still survives to demonstrate the architect's mastery of his craft and the characteristic features of the new style.

Also active in this period was Yury Velten (1730-1801), a prolific architect who designed many fine buildings. He was for many years credited with the planning of the famous Neva embankments, with their remarkable beauty of design and magnificence of scale; but the most recent research has shown that there is no basis for attributing this work to him. Nor is he any longer regarded as the designer of the famous grille round the Summer Garden in St Petersburg. He was responsible for the execution of these works in his capacity as chief architect of the "Building Department" which carried out all building operations in the capital. The real designer of the embankments and the grille has not yet been definitely established.

Much of the palace building carried out during these years was the work of Antonio Rinaldi (c. 1710-1794), an Italian architect who found a second home in Russia. Rinaldi's major achievement was the Chinese Palace at Oranienbaum (now Lomonosov), with lavish carved and painted decoration reminiscent of mid 18th century architecture. A much plainer building by the same architect is the Marble Palace in St Petersburg, a majestic structure faced with coloured marble and decorated with Corinthian pilasters. Certain decorative elements in this building still retain traces of the *rocaille* style of the late Rococo; but these are res-trained and unobtrusive and are subordinated to the severe lines of the over-all design. The interior of the Marble Palace is also decorated with marble car-ving by some of the leading Russian sculptors of the day, including Shubin and Kozlovsky. The characte-ristic feature of Rinaldi's buildings, including his Gatchina Palace, is his con-

centration on decoration and ornament: to him the problems involved in the general conception and design of a building were of secondary importance.

The work of the architects we have been considering thus shows all the evidence of belonging to a period of transition when a new type of Russian architecture was in process of development. The buildings they erected became an integral part of the architectural pattern of St Petersburg, Moscow and other cities, not only giving the period a distinctive style of its own but also preparing the way for the achievements of the leading architects of the following period — Bazhenov, Kazakov and Starov. In the work of these architects Russian classicism found its fullest expression, and the buildings they designed represent the culminating point of Russian architecture in the second half of the 18th century.

The most gifted of the three was Vasily Bazhenov (1737-99), an architect of outstanding talent and great professional accomplishment. He occupies a special place in the history of Russian architecture as a man of wide culture, an apostle of the philosophy of the Enlightenment, a scholar and theoretical writer, and a great teacher. After receiving his early training in Ukhtomsky's school in Moscow he soon found his way to St Petersburg and completed his professional education in the newly established Academy of Arts. Two years later he was sent to France and Italy, where he made a thorough study of classical architecture. The work he did during his stay in these countries revealed his considerable talent, and he was elected to membership of a number of European academies.

Returning to St Petersburg in 1765, he was appointed an Academician and prepared a design for a new Arsenal. He then went back to Moscow, and a new period of creative activity began. The most important work he produced during this period was a design for a palace in the Kremlin (1767-73). This was a grandiose plan for the erection of a great palace complex on the Kremlin hill, incorporating all the existing buildings into a pattern which included a number of open squares and grand colonnades. Bazhenov's design replaced the seclusion and privacy of the mid 18th century palaces by the new conception of a complex of buildings open to the public view. Much use was made of the Ionic order on the exterior of the palace, producing an effect of sober magnificence and monumentality. Bazhenov produced a superb model of his projected palace, which gives us some idea of the magnificence of his conception. The model is of particular value because the building was never in fact built: there was a ceremonial laying of the foundation stone, but the structure never progressed beyond this. Nevertheless Bazhenov's design had great influence on his contemporaries and made a major contribution towards establishing the principles of classicism in Russian architecture.

The principles of planning exemplified in this project represented an important and influential contribution to architectural design. Bazhenov showed equal originality in his design for a palace at Tsaritsyno on the outskirts of Moscow, in which, basing himself on the older traditions of Russian architecture, he planned a whole series of buildings to be sited in a park — an Imperial residence in the country consisting of two main ranges of buildings, together with various pavilions and summer-houses, domestic offices, a theatre and other associated buildings. The whole design is notable for its quiet elegance, the organic link between the architecture and the surrounding countryside, and the lavish decoration. Although the Empress Catherine wanted the palace to be in the Moorish Gothic style, Bazhenov followed the established traditions of Russian architecture, and it is this that gives his design its distinctive character.

The unfortunate architect, however, was dogged by misfortune. Catherine, suspecting him of a connection with the freemasons, declared the style of the building to be too sombre for her taste, had it razed to the ground, and commissioned Kazakov to design a new palace. Nevertheless the study of

Bazhenov's original designs — which fortunately have been preserved — and of the other buildings in the complex still enable us to appreciate the great merits of his work.

One of Bazhenov's finest buildings was the Pashkov Palace in Moscow (1786), now the Lenin Library. The plan of the building followed the typical layout of a noble establishment, with the mansion on top of the hill and the garden on the lower slopes, surrounded by a grille. The principal reception rooms were in the main block, with living quarters in pavilions round the outside. The general composition is extremely effective: standing in a commanding position on its hill, the building looks impressive from every direction. The principles of layout are entirely traditional, recalling the technique of the older Russian architects with their unerring instinct for the siting of architectural masses in the landscape. The Pashkov Palace was one of Bazhenov's finest achievements and a magnificent addition to the townscape of Moscow.

One of the last of Bazhenov's major works was the Michael Castle (Engineers' Castle) in St Petersburg, built for Paul I. This is in the form of a closed square with an internal courtyard, and the main decorative features are on the principal façade, to which a high plinth, a portico, twin columns and sculptured decoration give a particularly imposing effect. Bazhenov died before the building was finished, and the work was completed by the Italian architect Vincenzo Brenna. Brenna departed from Bazhenov's original plan and overloaded the building with decoration, but the general character of the design was preserved. In 1800 Rastrelli's equestrian statue of Peter the Great, made half a century earlier, was erected in the square in front of the castle, where it harmonised perfectly with the façade and greatly enhanced the effect of the building.

Bazhenov was an architect of authentic greatness, whose significance extends far beyond the bounds of his century. In his layouts and designs he not only contributed to the development of the classical style and gave it distinctively Russian characteristics, but anticipated many of the ideas which were to play a central part in the architecture of later generations.

Matvey Kazakov (1738-1812) was the second of the three great architects of this period. He too received his professional training in Ukhtomsky's studio in Moscow, and then practised as an architect in Tver. His architectural education was completed by Bazhenov, whom he assisted in the designing of the Kremlin palace. Kazakov's first important work was the Petrovsky Palace (begun 1775). The design of this building — the line of the façades and the general layout — was influenced by the traditions of Russian architecture, and also betrayed the influence of Bazhenov.

In the 1770s Kazakov built the so-called "Government Offices" in the Kremlin (now occupied by the Supreme Soviet). This was planned in the form of a triangle, one side of which faced on to Red Square, enclosing a grand courtyard; but it was also an entirely new type of administrative building, planned with great economy and functional efficiency.

Kazakov's originality and professional competence were also demonstrated by his design for Moscow University, built between 1786 and 1793. In style this building was much more restrained, and it showed a great advance in the use of the order. At the end of the 1790s Kazakov built the Golitsyn Hospital in Moscow — a large complex of buildings consisting of a central block flanked by wings containing the wards. The severe Doric porticoes and the central dome are very characteristic of his style.

The third great architect of the period was Ivan Starov (1774-1808), who was also trained in the Academy of Arts. His work covered a very wide range — palaces, public and administrative buildings, churches — and he was also much concerned with urban layout. The most important of his earlier works was the Cathedral of the Trinity in the Alexander Nevsky Monastery in St Petersburg. A three-aisled basilica in plan, the Cathedral has a severe Doric hexastyle portico and is crowned by a dome and two bell-towers. Even this early work showed Starov's remarkable gifts and in particular his understanding of the classical order.

In his later years Starov was responsible for a palace at Pella, a mansion on the estate of Sivoritsa (both on the outskirts of Leningrad), and other buildings; but his outstanding achievement was the Tauride Palace in St Petersburg (1783-89) *(Plate p. 161)*, built for Prince G. Potëmkin. In this building he adopts a severely classical style, incorporating the Doric order, observing strict restraint in the design of the main structure, and emphasising the flatness of the walls. The central block extends back from the façade, with the lateral wings enclosing a grand courtyard which is cut off from the street by a grille. The interior of the palace, the internal colonnades and the sculptured decoration are of superlative effect.

Bazhenov, Kazakov and Starov thus made a considerable mark on their period, producing buildings which not only demonstrated their own professional mastery but also made an outstanding contribution to Russian architecture and to the successful establishment of the principles of classicism.

These three architects did not, however, stand alone. Many others, both Russian and foreign, were active in this period, all making their contribution to the development of Russian architecture. Among them was Nikolay Lvov.

Nikolay Lvov (1751-1803), a man of wide culture — a poet, composer and scholar as well as a very gifted architect — is principally known as the designer of the Post Office in St Petersburg. The clearly articulated design of the basement storey, the severe pilasters on the first floor and the functional planning of the building demonstrate the architect's technical mastery and his remarkable sense of style. It was to buildings such as this that St Petersburg owed its severely classical lines and its unique beauty. Lvov is also known as the designer of the Neva Gate in the Fortress of SS. Peter and Paul, a work of classical restraint which harmonises perfectly with the plainness of the walls. Lvov's activities were not, however, confined to St Petersburg: among the many buildings outside the capital for which he was responsible the most important is the cathedral in Torzhok, a large building in the classical style with five domes.

The Italian architect Giacomo Quarenghi (1744-1817) was another foreigner who found a second home in Russia, coming to St Petersburg in 1779 and remaining there until his death. He was well versed in the traditions of Russian architecture, which had a great influence on his work and played a part in the design of many buildings which gave clear expression to the principles of Russian classicism.

One of Quarenghi's early works was the Academy of Science in St Petersburg, situated on the banks of the Neva (1787). The pillared portico, the clearly defined granite basement storey and the staircase leading to the main entrance underline the restrained simplicity of the design of the façade.

From the beginning Quarenghi's work shows a striving towards sobriety of form and the most effective use of the order. During the 1780s he also built the Hermitage Theatre, fitting it so skilfully into the architectural ensemble on the Neva embankment that in spite of the difference in style it combined with the Winter Palace to form a unified whole. Here again Quarenghi emphasises the separateness of the basement storey, linking the two upper stories with a Corinthian colonnade.

All Quarenghi's work shows the same delicacy of proportion in the details — the doors and windows, the cornices, and so on. One of his most important buildings is the Assignation Bank in Sadovy Street, a complex and skilfully designed structure consisting of a central block linked by an open colonnade to a long semicircular gallery. In the central block the Corinthian order is used.

Quarenghi's mastery was also displayed in the English Palace at Peterhof and the Aleksandrovsky Palace at Pushkin. Unfortunately the English Palace was destroyed by German forces during the second world war, but the Aleksandrovsky Palace is still one of the attractions of the town of Pushkin, merging harmoniously into the park in which it is set. This easy harmony between the palace and the park is largely due to the splendid double colonnade in the Corinthian order which links the projecting elements of the building. The colonnade itself is a masterpiece of architectural skill.

Quarenghi also designed many buildings in the suburbs of St Petersburg, as well as in Moscow and other towns. The classical sobriety and formality of his work was very much in the spirit of the time, and the buildings he designed stood out even in a period of great architectural achievement as a permanent contribution to the architectural heritage of Russia.

Another foreigner who occupies a prominent place in the history of Russian architecture is the Scottish architect Charles Cameron (1740s to 1812), who did much work in the immediate surroundings of St Petersburg, including in particular the Agate Pavilion, the Hanging Gardens and the galleries at Tsarskoe Selo (now Pushkin) and a palace at Pavlovsk. Cameron's style is seen at its best in the interiors of his palaces, where the intricate design of moulded ornament and parquet flooring offered scope for his exquisite taste and his delicate sense of style.

Among many other architects who did good work during this period were Vincenzo Brenna, Egor Sokolov and Ivan Egorov.

The last thirty years of the 18th century were thus a period of great achievement in the history of Russian architecture. They were also a time of remarkable progress in urban development, during which new principles of town planning were established and great advances were made in the art of landscape gardening.

Thus Russian art could look back on a long and fruitful course of development during the 18th century, a period of steady advance and great achievement. The century was notable for the establishment of a new materialistic ideology, the abandonment of the old mediaeval dogmas, and the creation of a secular and realistic school of art. This process had begun in an earlier century, but it acquired a particular impetus and direction in the Petrine period.

Religious art did not, however, disappear in the 18th century: it was neither destroyed nor prohibited. As in earlier times, icons were painted and churches were decorated; as in earlier times, the building of churches continued, and successive generations of craftsmen devoted their skill to handing on the traditions of these older arts. But in the new conditions religious art lost its former pre-eminence, retreated before the advance of secular art, and underwent significant change. The whole of religious art came under the influence of the trend towards realism, and icon-painting increasingly lost its former monumentality and schematism.

The vigorous forward movement of Russian art and its full measure of achievement were demonstrated in many ways, not least in the high standards of professional skill attained by Russian artists and craftsmen. Rejecting the conventionality and schematism of mediaeval views on artistic creation, they gained a new vision of the world, a new conception of the rôle of art in human life, a new understanding of form.

Russian art reflected the enhanced significance now accorded to human personality, in fundamental contrast to the mediaeval attitude. Man now achieved a deeper understanding of the world around him, no longer seeking in it manifestations of the divine will but rather striving to use it for his own purposes and bring it under the control of human reason.

The realistic approach which now became the dominant strain in Russian art led to the emergence of new genres, which previously had either not existed or had not developed beyond a rudimentary stage. Portrait painting advanced to a leading position; its aim was now to reveal the inmost essence of human personality, to establish its individual validity and its independence of any association with class, to demonstrate its manysidedness and its profound significance.

Russian art, as exemplified particularly in architecture, sculpture and historical painting, was permeated with a consciousness of human rights and obligations, a mood of patriotic fervour, a sense of social duty — trends which were to be further developed in the following century. This concern with human rights and duties was a consequence of the increasing national and social awareness of Russian society, the further strengthening of government organisation, and the advance of the Enlightenment.

The foreign artists who came to Russia at the beginning of the 18th century occupied a place of some prominence in the artistic life of the country. They found a ready market for their talents and achieved a degree of prosperity which was denied to the Russian artists of the day. In the second half of the century, however, the situation underwent a radical change. The artists turned out by the new Academy of Arts rapidly demonstrated their superiority and obtained European recognition; and Russian artists now began to be entrusted with commissions of increasing importance and to give striking evidence of their high standards of professional accomplishment.

The distinctive characteristic of 18th century Russian art is the urgent pace of its advance. Never before had the various genres developed so rapidly; never before had new and progressive ideas obtained such ready acceptance over so wide a field.

LIST OF ILLUSTRATIONS

90 Suzdal: Church of the Resurrection. 1720. (Ph. Novosti).

91 Zagorsk: icon of the Virgin, with oklad of silver inlaid with precious stones. 18th century. (Ph. G. Bertin).

92 Arkhangelskoe: Church of St Michael, on the banks of the River Moskva. 18th century. (Ph. G. Bertin).

93 Carved wooden figure of a man. Early 18th century. Museum, Pereslavl-Zalessky. (Ph. Novosti).

94 Artist unknown. Portrait of Ivan Turgenev. Early 18th century. Russian Museum, Leningrad. (Ph. Novosti).

95 Roman Nikitin. Portrait of Madame Stroganov. Early 18th century. Hermitage Museum, Leningrad. (Ph. Novosti).

96 Ivan Nikitin. Portrait of Peter the Great. Early 18th century. Russian Museum, Leningrad. (Ph. Novosti).

97 Ivan Nikitin. Portrait of a hetman (a senior Cossack officer). 1730. Russian Museum, Leningrad. (Ph. Novosti).

99 Moscow: sleigh belonging to the Empress Elizabeth. Armoury, Kremlin. 18th century. (Ph. G. Bertin).

100 Zagorsk: candelabrum. 18th century. (Ph. G. Bertin).

101 The same.

102 Tsarskoe Selo (Pushkin): Catherine Palace, designed by Bartolommeo Rastrelli. 1752-1756. (Ph. J. Goetelen).

105 The same.

108 St Petersburg (Leningrad): the Winter Palace (now the Hermitage Museum), designed by Bartolommeo Rastrelli. 1755-1762. (Ph. J. Goetelen).

109 The same: throne-room, restored by Vasily Stasov in 1837. (Ph. J. Goetelen).

110 St Petersburg (Leningrad): Smolny Convent. 1746-1757. (Ph. J. Goetelen).

111 St Petersburg (Leningrad): cathedral in Smolny Convent, designed by Bartolommeo Rastrelli. 1746-1757. (Ph. J. Goetelen).

112 St Petersburg (Leningrad): façade of Cathedral of St Nicholas, designed by Savva Chevakinsky. 1753-1762. (Ph. J. Goetelen).

113 St Petersburg (Leningrad): interior of Cathedral of St Nicholas. 1753-1762. (Ph. J. Goetelen).

114 St Petersburg (Leningrad): bell-tower of Cathedral of St Nicholas. 1753-1762. (Ph. J. Goetelen).

115 Zagorsk: bell-tower of Monastery of the Trinity and St Sergius, designed by D. Ukhtomsky. 1741-1770. (Ph. G. Bertin).

116 Kuskovo: the Grotto. 1755-1775. (Ph. G. Bertin).

117 The same: the Dutch House. 1749. (Ph. G. Bertin).

118 The same: façade of palace. 1769-1775. (Ph. G. Bertin).

119 The same: the French park. 18th century. (Ph. G. Bertin).

120 The same: the Hermitage. 1765-1767. (Ph. G. Bertin).

123 The same: tiled stove. 18th century. (Ph. G. Bertin).

124 Moscow: façade of Ostankino Palace, formerly the residence of the Counts Sheremetev. 18th century. (Ph. J.-P. Gaume).

125 Moscow: colonnade in theatre, Ostankino Palace. End of 18th century. (Ph. G. Bertin).

126–127 Moscow: interior of Ostankino Palace. 18th century. (Ph. Novosti).

128 Carlo Rastrelli. Statue of the Empress Anna. 1741. Russian Museum, Leningrad. (Ph. Novosti).

129 Moscow: detail of inlaid parquet flooring in Ostankino Palace. (Ph. G. Bertin).

131 Arkhangelskoe: ballroom in palace. End of 18th century.

132 Fëdor Rokotov. Portrait of Vasily Maykov. 1765. Tretyakov Gallery, Moscow. (Ph. Novosti).

133 Arkhangelskoe: the palace and the park. End of 18th century. (Ph. G. Bertin).

134 Ivan Vishnyakov. Portrait of Sarah Fermor. About 1750. Russian Museum, Leningrad. (Ph. Novosti).

135 Aleksey Antropov. Portrait of Ataman Krasnoshchekov. 1761. Russian Museum, Leningrad. (Ph. Novosti).

136 Fëdor Rokotov. Portrait of Madame Santi. 1785. Russian Museum, Leningrad. (Ph. Novosti).

137 Dmitry Levitsky. Portrait of Aleksandr Kokorinov. 1770. Russian Museum, Leningrad. (Ph. Novosti).

139 Dmitry Levitsky. Portrait of Diderot. 1773. Museum of Art and History, Geneva. (Ph. G. Bertin).

141 Vladimir Borovikovsky. Portrait of Mademoiselle Lopukhin. 1797. Tretyakov Gallery, Moscow. (Ph. Novosti).

145 Vladimir Borovikovsky. Portrait of Mademoiselle Arsenyev. About 1790. Tretyakov Gallery, Moscow. (Ph. Novosti).

149 Fedot Shubin. Bust of I. Schwarz. Marble. 1792. Russian Museum, Leningrad. (Ph. Novosti).

150 *Fedot Shubin. Bust of Lomonosov. Marble. 1790. Academy of Science, Moscow. (Ph. Novosti).*

151 *Fedot Shubin. Bust of Paul I. Marble. 1801. Russian Museum, Leningrad. (Ph. Novosti).*

152 *Mikhail Kozlovsky. Monument to General Suvorov. 1801. Leningrad. (Ph. Novosti).*

155 *St Petersburg (Leningrad): Monument to Peter the Great, by Etienne Falconet. 1782. (Ph. J. Goetelen).*

157 *St Petersburg (Leningrad): the Mint. 1742; restored in 19th century. (Ph. J. Goetelen).*

158 *Suzdal: Church of St Nicholas. 1766. (Ph. M. Shavranov).*

159 *The same.*

161 *St Petersburg (Leningrad): Tauride Palace, designed by Ivan Starov. 1783-1789. (Ph. J. Goetelen).*

172

CONTENTS

PRINTED IN FEBRUARY 1968
ON THE PRESSES OF NAGEL PUBLISHERS, GENEVA

THE BINDING WAS EXECUTED
IN THE WORKSHOPS OF NAGEL PUBLISHERS, GENEVA

PLATES IN BLACK AND WHITE AND IN COLOUR
ENGRAVED BY CLICHÉS UNION, PARIS

THE PUBLISHER'S LEGAL DEPOSIT NUMBER IS 444

PRINTED IN SWITZERLAND